Writing in Coffee Shops

Writing in Coffee Shops

Confessions of
a Playwright

Ryan Craig

BLOOMSBURY ACADEMIC
NEW YORK • LONDON • OXFORD • NEW DELHI • SYDNEY

METHUEN DRAMA
Bloomsbury Publishing Plc
50 Bedford Square, London, WC1B 3DP, UK
1385 Broadway, New York, NY 10018, USA
29 Earlsfort Terrace, Dublin 2, Ireland

BLOOMSBURY, METHUEN DRAMA and the Methuen Drama logo are trademarks of
Bloomsbury Publishing Plc

First published in Great Britain 2021

Cover design by Charlotte Daniels
Cover images: Paper © Alamy / iStock, yellow sticky notes
© Chinch / Shutterstock

A catalogue record for this book is available from the British Library.

Library of Congress Cataloging-in-Publication Data
Names: Craig, Ryan, 1972 January 9- author.
Title: Writing in coffee shops : confessions of a playwright / Ryan Craig.
Description: New York : Bloomsbury Academic, 2021. | Summary: "What makes someone
a playwright? How do their identities and ideas interweave and co-exist? What permanent
truths can we discern from examining existing texts? How can we write theatre that
encapsulates the contemporary moment? How do we develop an idea from the embryonic
impulse to a full and robust piece of theatre? In this fresh, lively and often very funny book,
playwright Ryan Craig makes a case for the vitality of playwriting in our contemporary world
and offers a way into writing those plays. From the very first moment of the process, as
you sit in a coffee shop, staring at your 'laptop yawning open like some big, gormless
mouth, the screen a flickering blank', to seeing your play staged and reviewed, the author
takes you through the complete journey. Drawing on his own experience of writing for
theatres such as the National, Hampstead and Tricycle and Menier Chocolate Factory,
TV drama scripts for BBC, ITV and Channel Four, radio plays and adaptation, as well as
commercial theatre, the author explores what practical tools the dramatist can use to write
plays that build bridges between us. Full of practical advice for the aspiring – and practising
– playwright, this book is also an important call-to-arms for playwrights everywhere, arguing
for its necessity in the context of an increasingly fractured, distracted, disconnected
world"—Provided by publisher.
Identifiers: LCCN 2020045157 (print) | LCCN 2020045158 (ebook) |
ISBN 9781350190849 (paperback) | ISBN 9781350190832 (hardback) |
ISBN 9781350190856 (ePDF) | ISBN 9781350190870 (eBook)
Subjects: LCSH: Playwriting. | Drama—Technique.
Classification: LCC PN1661 .C73 2021 (print) | LCC PN1661 (ebook) | DDC 808.2—dc23
LC record available at https://lccn.loc.gov/2020045157
LC ebook record available at https://lccn.loc.gov/2020045158

ISBN: HB: 978-1-3501-9083-2
       PB: 978-1-3501-9084-9
       ePDF: 978-1-3501-9085-6
       eBook: 978-1-3501-9087-0

Typeset by RefineCatch Limited, Bungay, Suffolk
Printed and bound in Great Britain

To find out more about our authors and books visit www.bloomsbury.com
and sign up for our newsletters.

For Lew

Contents

Introduction

We are at war. As I write this, Western civilisation is in the midst of a bitter struggle for its cultural soul. How do we balance the important new social sensitivities with our hard-won creative freedoms? Who has the right to tell which story, why and in what way? What is the purpose of art and can it ever really be free from the political exigencies of our tumultuous times? The theatre has always regarded itself as a force for opposition: a force against intolerance, against oppression, against complacency, but now it seems to be a force in opposition to itself. We're going through a collective identity crisis: a catechising of our embedded orthodoxies, a soul-searching over deeply held assumptions about an artist's entitlements, about the limits of the imagination, about the nature of authenticity, and this sustained offensive against our traditional beliefs is having a profound effect on how we consider, construct, programme and produce new work for our stages.

To anyone paying attention, the current revolution should not come as a complete surprise. Our cultural structures are so deeply rooted in our murky Patriarchal past that their dismantlement feels like a necessary purging. In the last few years our theatres have been bursting with the brilliant work of young, iconoclastic playwrights: Alice Birch, Annie Baker, Branden Jacobs-Jenkins, Laura Wade, Lucy Prebble, Lucy Kirkwood, Ella Hickson, Ella Road, Ruby Thomas, Alexander Zeldin, Jackie Sibblies Drury, Jasmine Lee-Jones, the list goes on. Writers whose plays are explicitly bulldozing through these old structures, challenging or subverting or sometimes even obliterating theatrical form in the process. Their writing displays a supreme confidence in their own dramatic voice. They are confronting head-on the question of what a play is or can be or should be or will be in the future.

All this prompts me to ask three questions in return. Can we isolate some universal principles of dramatic writing that are true for all plays and all time? What is the playwright's place in this new and turbulent world beyond the theatre? How do we reach out and connect to the wider society and build a contemporary drama that exists for everyone?

No meaningful, living theatre has ever been divorced from the socio-political currents of its time. The atomisation of our digitised, phone-dominated lives has made the collective reception of story even more essential. Similarly, a perception that neo-liberalism has failed us, that institutions have failed us, that the future is more uncertain that ever, that our economy and our news organisations and our social foundations and our planet are under the severest threat have led us to query every nut and bolt that held it all together. It's also led to the resurgence of a radicalism that's pushing us further and further apart and that means it's more vital than ever to bring people together to witness universal truths about our shared humanity in a shared space and at a shared time. But there seems to be a question about where precisely the battle lines should be drawn.

In this age of disruption and disassembling it's no wonder writers are trying to liberate themselves from the tyranny of conventional dramatic structure. Indeed, theatre makers appear to be asking whether we are entering a new era that is emancipated from narrative altogether. But if all artistic achievement, from the Upper Palaeolithic cave paintings to Jacques-Louis David's *Death of Marat*, from *The Pardoner's Tale* to *Casablanca* to *seven methods of killing kylie jenner*, somehow contains the same creative DNA, and evolves from the same universal human need to represent and connect, wouldn't it therefore be counter-intuitive to completely vanquish the fundamentals of dramatic storytelling? For one thing these fundamentals have shaped the development of our brains, shaped the way we perceive the world and our place in it.

Can we really survive in a void? Surely you need the rules to exist in order to break them. Surely you need to understand the structures in order to change them. 'To have a culture', said Arthur Miller, 'you have to have a past'. In 1992 Albanians were revolting against decades of tyranny and isolationism (many were not aware the Berlin Wall had fallen until long after). People took to the streets and smashed everything that reminded them of their communist past. They didn't just demolish statues and monuments, they didn't just throw out politicians, they wrecked totally factories and schools, greenhouses, and hospitals, they tore down fences and tore up water pipes. Everything, the entire infrastructure, was seen as a symbol of their enslavement. The leaders of the new Democratic Party and the police simply stood by and watched. 'Is this,' wrote the Croatian journalist Slavenka Drakulić, 'how they understood freedom: as the freedom to destroy?' Drakulić was sympathetic. She saw a people for so many years cut off from the world, saturated in fear, and then seduced by images of Western plenty. Unlike other post-communist countries, Albania wanted so much to expunge their past they left themselves no foundations on which to build their future. 'The ultimate price of isolation and naiveté was high,' Drakulić continued, 'a kind of self-destruction. It was as if Albanians believed that a nation or an individual could start life from point zero.'

In my view an annihilation of classic dramatic structure would be tantamount to a kind of cultural patricide that could leave us intellectually orphaned and teetering on the top of a dangerously collapsible scaffold. Think of it this way: if a friend decided one day to entirely deny their genetic ancestry, to eradicate their collective memory, wouldn't we see this as a damaging assault on their unconscious and stage an urgent intervention?

This book intends to be part of that intervention. By exploring what makes someone a playwright, how their identities and ideas interweave and co-exist and what permanent truths we can discern from examining existing texts, it will expose the connecting tissue between the writer's life, their art and the world in which they live.

Currently the deeper substance of a writer's make-up is being neglected by a system that covets the 'cool' and the 'relevant' and the 'sexy' and other empty slogans usually deployed by people who are demonstrably none of these things. A system that fetishises youth and commodifies identity will make false gods of artists whom it will inevitably betray. This system serves us in only the shallowest of ways. What happens when the young get older or when someone from a minority background wants to explore themes and characters outside their experience? How will we support them over their careers when the 'relevance' of their identity or their youth gives way, as it inevitably must, to the next generation? Why not nurture and develop and deepen the talent that made their work sing?

If we're to remould the theatre in our own contemporary image we must straddle opposing points: past and future, convention and invention, respect and irreverence. When I was growing up in the eighties I used to love the comedian Les Dawson. Not the terrible mother-in-law jokes, but the regular segment in his act where he'd play the piano badly on purpose. As he played he'd cheerfully exhort the audience to join in with an old standard like *Side by Side* or *Me and My Girl*, waving an arm in increasingly frantic encouragement, desperately grinning as the audience's hopeless attempt to follow the tortured melody quickly collapsed and the whole thing came crashing in on itself. It was a sublimely funny routine (YouTube it if you want to make up your own mind about that), and the reason it worked was that Dawson was actually an expert pianist. He could play the piece so well he was able to pinpoint which notes to get wrong and precisely when and precisely how wrong to get them – a semitone higher or lower, inserted at the end of a musical phrase or halfway through it – so he could wring the most humour out of this apparently hapless incompetence. Dawson's skill here was in connecting two seemingly separate points: his own sense of childish wonder and mischief, and his technical prowess and proficiency. What he knew is that without the marriage of these two opposites the idea would not take flight. He knew the rules before he broke them.

Similarly Picasso knew how to draw figurative representations of objects before he painted *Guernica* or *The Women of Algiers* and reinvented the way we see the world. Barbara Hepworth learned how to carve marble into recognisable shapes before she created her iconic megaliths with those erotic holes, and Renzo Piano and Richard Rogers could design a garden shed before they designed the Pompidou Centre.

A balance, then, must be struck between holding on to universal precepts and the invention of new ones. Indeed, all playwrights have a touch of the funambulist in them. Writing for the theatre is always a tightrope act. Instead of a safety net there's a group of scribblers with 500-word deadlines waiting for you to fall. What's more, writing that challenges the status quo, which the playwright is duty-bound to do, is always precarious. Turning your face against the acceptable standards of ethics and good taste will always single you out for attack. Paul Verlaine exhorted us to *'grab hold of eloquence and twist off its neck!'* and if the new play elicits hostility and suspicion it's probably doing its job. The playwright has to find his or her or their own truth and deliver it in as raw and pointed a way as possible, whatever the cost. Anything else is just howling in the night. But at a time when ideology, outrage and censoriousness have calcified debate (were things this prickly for Ibsen when he eviscerated the suffocating moral hypocrisy of nineteenth-century Norway?) it is understandable why theatre-makers would be drawn to working in a collective. Devised work, multi-discipline artist collaborations, verbatim reportage, film and book adaptations, all these can lead to the creation of great art and wonderful nights in the theatre. But this kind of work is easier to love and harder to fear. It must never replace the lone voice: the singular, uncompromising mind tying technique to imagination and presenting a unique vision to a group of strangers. When an individual reaches out through the prism of dramatic art in pursuit of some deep, human truth, that work can become a solitary light in the darkness.

The shining of this light is, to my mind, the theatre's sacred purpose. Staged drama can be a beacon for our society, can lead the mainstream to better things. If it abnegates this responsibility, uncouples from the majority and sets off on its own into the far horizon, the theatre will head into an ever-decreasing, self-regarding death spiral. A play must speak to everyone, across all strata. That's how it affects change.

Indeed, the next few years will be crucial in determining how we emerge from the total upheaval we're living through and what the future looks like. In the age of social-media echo chambers it's even more important for us to say the unsayable about the human condition. How we can achieve this through drama is the mission of this book.

I need to add here, of course, that much of this book has been written from lockdown where the only show in town is coronavirus: this virulently infectious plague so swiftly and overwhelmingly laid waste to our economy and cultural life that it has forced the theatre, as we understood it, into a frozen exile. But while it might seem odd to be writing a book about writing in coffee shops when, at the beginning of this crisis there were no coffee shops to write *in* and no theatres to write *for*, it's even more urgent for us to fight for the kind of theatre we want to see in the world when we do finally emerge into the brave new dawn.

I believe that in this time of confusion, when we're all looking into the dark unknown and wondering what's coming towards us, playwrights can make a significant contribution. It's in the nature of our job to co-exist with uncertainty and contradiction. It's a precarious profession: to do it, you need nerves of steel and a natural ability to constantly adapt to the changing tides. The work is done in private and yet delivered in public so a playwright's personality tends to have to accommodate opposing characteristics. They have to be solitary, yet garrulous: obsessive about the detail yet relaxed in collaboration: alert to the cultural mores of the day yet belligerently contrarian: tolerant of peoples' fatal frailties and wild idiosyncrasies and yet deeply attached to universal truths about the human condition.

So, using my own experience of writing for various platforms: plays for the National Theatre or Hampstead Theatre or Menier Chocolate Factory, drama scripts for the BBC, ITV and Channel 4, radio plays, adaptation and commercial theatre, I'm going to explore both the particular psychology and the practical tools the dramatist can use to build bridges between us while all around they're being gleefully incinerated. How do we develop an idea from the embryonic impulse to a full and robust piece of theatre? Ideas and the very human contradictions and imperfections that impel them into existence are what incite and define our plays, but they need an internal structure to exist for them to awaken and take flight. How we recognise, evolve and apply these internal structures is where we're going to start.

1 Idea

Here's the secret about writing drama. Everything you need to know, you already know. Not only that, you've known it for years. When you were five you knew how to tell a story, you knew how to make it dramatically active. You'd start by saying *'the most amazing thing happened today'*, because you already knew how to hook the listener's interest, how to create anticipation, how to create suspense. You'd say *'I saw the biggest, angriest dog in the world'*, because, instinctively, you knew how to characterise, how to embellish, how to manipulate that mental image, how to make it extraordinary and not ordinary. You'd say *'then'*, because you unconsciously understood progression, *'then'*, you'd repeat, sensitive to the concept of driving tension, of rhythm, *'then, I saw this little boy went right up to the dog . . . and . . . and he put his hand right in his mouth'*, because you knew, even at this formative age, how to grip the listener, how to hold their attention by dragging the story into the present tense, by raising the stakes, by introducing the possibility of something called *consequence*: the possibility of something *happening*, something that would *affect* the life of the individual involved. And this interior, inbuilt sense of suspense and embellishment, of rhythm and consequence, allowed you to build a natural structure to your story, a beginning, middle and end. *'And then'*, you say, reaching your climax and going for the jugular, approaching the killer moment, the moment the audience will lean forward, will hold their breath in expectation, *'then, the dog bit down'*. And you pause, sensing the anticipation you created within that suspended silence will make the listener lean forward even more, before bringing the tale to its breathless conclusion with *'And right at the last minute, the boy pulled his hand away'*. And there we have the denouement and the resolution and all of this you knew without having been specifically *taught*, without reading any *books*, without going on any *courses* or even studying any *plays*. You knew then and you *know* now because we are all engineered to tell dramatic narratives.

'The creative writer', said Freud in his 1907 lecture *The Creative Writer and Daydreaming*, 'acts no differently from the child at play, he creates a fantasy world, which he takes very seriously'. Equally, 'every child at play behaves like a writer … by imposing a new and more pleasing order on the things that make up his world'.

Simply put, we're made this way. We take the events we experience and reorganise them around a specific pulse and meter, we use the appropriate rhythms and tempos, naturally rising and falling like music. It's how we connect and communicate, how we inform or entertain or warn or console, how we make sense of the absurdities and contradictions of life, of death, of sex, of politics. It's a vital skill necessary to assert and maintain our place in society. Until only a few thousand years ago keeping that place in the tribe was crucial to our survival, for it was the tribe that sustained and protected us – and that innate capacity to connect to others, to illicit their attention and sympathy by weaving a dramatic narrative out of lived experience is still hard-wired into us today.

But if that's true, why am I stuck? Why am I sitting in this coffee shop, laptop yawning open like some big, gormless mouth, the screen a flickering blank? Why am I staring into space, wondering where I go from here? I only have a few hours this morning to write. Later I'm meant to be to dropping in on 'tech' rehearsals for my latest play, *Games For Lovers*, which opens at 'The Vaults' in less than a week. My stomach's churning with a mixture of dread and excitement: the thought of all those capable people building a working theatre in a vast black tubular cavity underneath Waterloo Station: the thought of the actors limbering up their bodies and climbing on top of their lines: the thought of that charged hush as the lights dim and the audience collectively encounters a new story, a new set of characters for the very first time. I've had around fifteen new plays produced, several revivals, but the emotions are just as raw as they were the very first time.

Techs are notoriously tense occasions: the director is effectively implanting a set of technical markers, lighting cues, sound cues, props settings and stage management choreography, as a framework for the performance. Naturally the actors and the crew are highly focused on this exercise, as it gets them through the show night after night, and the writer is absolutely the last person anyone needs hanging about. I'll slip in to the back like the ghost at the feast and watch director Anthony Banks and sound designer Ben Ringham in some power huddle like a shorts-and-black-t-shirt-clad Nixon and Kissinger plotting their high-stakes geopolitical manoeuvres. There'll be scaffolding and flats and props and boxes and people clambering up rigging, and painting walls and floors, and spotting lights. There'll be actors shuttling about half-costumed, panicked, excited, joking, intense, front-of-house staff setting up, producers dealing with some broken ego or a last-minute marketing crisis, the atmosphere will be electric, everyone pulsating with activity and purpose. But the writer? An appendage. My work long over, I'm now relegated to a dangling bystander, little more than a useless, hunk of scenery long since struck from the final blueprints and now getting under everyone's feet and wondering what the hell I'd started.

First, though, I need to get going on this book. The one you're reading right now. The kind of book I wished someone would've written before I had, in fact, 'started'. I once met the eminent playwright Timberlake Wertenbaker and her very first words to me have lingered ever since. 'If you knew', she asked, 'at the beginning of your career, what you know now, would you ever have started?' The question might sound like a test of loyalty or seriousness or even sanity, but it gets right to the core of the business of being a playwright. What the seasoned playwright knew was that it's impossible to separate your inner character from the work. As I've said, the job is a hazardous juggling act, an occupation of stark opposites. The intense isolation when writing is blown to smithereens by the joyous mucking together of rehearsal and the acutely public and often very bruising exposure of performance. It's this paradoxical existence I'm going to explore in this book, while at the same time living it in reality. Before that can happen though I need to get some words down: I need to do my job. Before *that* can happen, I need another coffee.

At the counter of the coffee shop I bump into another dad from my children's school. I don't know this person well and we have, what has become, a common interchange with those outside the theatre. Civilians.

'So what do you do exactly?'
'I'm a playwright'.
'Oh. That's...'
'Yeah'.
'Yeah'.
Awkward silence.
'So where do you get your ideas from?'

I used to scoff at this question, but it's not as inane as it sounds. When it comes to writing plays having ideas and knowing what to do with them is, as our American cousins might say, 'the whole ballgame'. What precisely *is* 'an idea'? Where, in fact, *do* you get them from and how do you know when one arrives? Can you fit your brain with an alarm system that'll go off when one appears? I'm sure I'm not the first person to imagine the existence of *An Ideas Shop*. Some shambling, musty, Dickensian outlet tucked away down a concealed side-street in Clapham Junction or Camden or Clerkenwell or Camberwell with its cluttered shelves oozing with hoards of 'ideas', and we could just pop along whenever we're stuck and we've got a new play to write and pick one up for a song. Sadly such a place does not exist. But even if it did, there's the more pressing question of how we would nurture and cultivate an idea from a mere concept into a concrete and unique work of art, of how we would impose our distinctive imprimatur on a subject. Because how we do this is what defines us as writers.

We humans are developmental creatures: our bodies and minds are constantly in flux. Look in the mirror and watch the tiny, daily changes happening to your face: the additional creases and cracks every time you laugh or frown, the battering your skin gets in the wind and rain, or a blast of UV from the sun. Why should it be any different for your imagination, with the cumulative experiences and emotions your brain processes every second? Even the way we think and use language is an organic and evolving thing.

The American philosopher Jerry Fodor believes our thoughts develop the same way language does. In his book *The Language of Thought* he says ideas have an intrinsic linguistic syntax. Simple concepts combine in systematic ways like grammatical rules, and then evolve into complex structures.

Think again about that five-year-old 'you'. Your dramatic instincts are raw and true, yes, but they need honing. Your five-year-old brain was a sponge and you were learning language at a rate of knots and through a combination of mimicry and guesswork. You heard the people around you speak and you began to construct a system, developing your language skills over time, so that each time you learned a new word you'd apply that system. So one day you'll say 'those two men *fight-ed* yesterday'. Only later do you learn to apply the exception to the rule so that you replace *fight-ed* with *fought* as the past participle. We realise fast how slippery and treacherous our language can be, how plastic and flexible, so our minds move like quicksilver to grasp it, to gain control of its complexities, because it's how we make ourselves understood. How we assert ourselves in the world.

How we *survive* in it. We do the same with ideas. One thought graduates to another more layered one as it collects new information over time: as it connects to some separate thought or memory, mutating into a more dynamic structure. And that dynamic, multi-layered, complex thought is what we need in order to start our play.

Here's what happens when you have an idea. A neuron sends a signal across your brain: a vibration, like a slinky toy being twanged and sending a shock wave into the stem on the left side of the brain where the buried memories swirl. A fragment from some memory or understanding or image makes contact with some other image or memory and forms a structure with multiple dimensions. This thought impulse happens unconsciously. You never actually think 'I must begin to have a thought', rather you find yourself *having* it. A thought isn't consciously harvested, but emerges into your consciousness before you realise it, like a character materialising on stage in front of your eyes.

Indeed, the thought may arrive as a character. They pop into your head and demand to be heard. They have a story to tell that could be dramatic, moving, funny, disturbing. We'll need to ascertain certain things. Who are they? What do they want? How do they speak and what do they have to say? Where have they come from? Stoppard famously said, 'every exit is an entrance somewhere else', and if that's the case every entrance is an exit *from* somewhere else. So their arrival suggests the existence of a concrete place. Great. Setting and character seem to be developing simultaneously, the two rubbing up against each other creating friction. An idea is beginning to take shape.

Clearing out my study recently I stumbled across a scrap of paper I'd been using as a bookmark. On it, scribbled in red ink, was a list of titles.

Game Theory
The Game

Fourteen Games About Love
Fourteen Games/Sixteen Games
Sixteen Games About Fucking
Games For Lovers and Non Lovers
Sweet Vitriol
Some Games
Sweet Liars
Live Games
The Game Play
Some Games Are Brutal

Some of these are a little embarrassing yes, but you can see the theme I'm going for.

In 2012, after my play *The Holy Rosenbergs* was produced in the National's Cottesloe space (now called the Dorfman), I was invited to become the Writer-in-Residence at the National Theatre Studio. The Studio is a 1950s building just up the road from the South Bank that was used as a set-painting and dressing workshop for Old Vic productions next door. It was subsequently converted in the 1960s into a rehearsal and office space for the nascent National Theatre. It's now a rarefied place. A hub for theatre practitioners of all stripes to try things out, to think, to experiment, to put stuff on its feet, to share ideas, it's a sort of theatre laboratory. It's had some snazzy refurbishments in recent years but when I was starting out it was pretty rough and ready. As a writer in my late twenties I was dumped in a cramped and oddly fragranced room on the second floor next to the gents' loos called 'the kitchen' where, I was assured, a number of extremely celebrated authors had penned their modern masterworks. My own effort, *What We Did To Weinstein*, was written on loose sheets of blank, unlined paper in about ten days and essentially kicked off my career.

Through the Studio I've made life-long friends and colleagues, developed my work and my voice with the help of the some of the best directors and actors on the planet, co-founded a fairly influential writers movement (more of which later), watched some extraordinary work in its formative stages and met some fascinating people. In a single day I remember encountering Richard Griffiths, Barbara Windsor and the Krankies. Ex-Labour leader Neil Kinnock even came in to read a few small roles in the workshop for a play about the NHS and at lunch told a hilarious yarn about when he got sun-burned on a tuna trawler after drinking too much (I think it was tequila and it was in Cuba but I couldn't swear to it), stumbled back to his hotel room to drench himself in soothing after-sun, only to be awoken by Glenys shrieking at the sight of him. He'd used bronzing cream instead of after-sun and his head was now glowing in the dark. In 2010, I spent a few extremely happy and productive weeks there finishing the final draft of *The Holy Rosenbergs* in a small room looking out on the comings and goings of the social housing estate on The Cut, while in the room abutting mine Tori Amos was composing songs for *The Light Princess* on the piano and singing as she went. That's the NT Studio.

While I was Writer-In-Residence, the Studio's then-head, Laura Collier, challenged me to use the time to do something I wouldn't ordinarily think of doing: write a romantic comedy for the stage. She organised workshops with actors, a director and musicians and we discussed and then improvised various different scenarios: bad dates, meet-ups, breaks-ups and make-ups. Eventually I had a notebook full of stories, characters and incidents. What I didn't have was an idea for a play. The crucial breakthrough came a few weeks later when, inspired by the director Ria Parry's drama exercises during the workshops, I returned to Augusto Boal's *Games For Actors and Non Actors*. In that book he talks about his experiments with Forum Theatre. The performers in Boal's shows interact with their audiences and employ drama techniques to discuss issues relevant to their lives. Reading this it occurred to me that the *games* we play in love might relate to the theatre games we use in workshops and rehearsals. Perhaps this could be the connecting thread around which the characters and stories could coalesce.

An 'idea', then, is a complex, evolving organism rather than a light-bulb moment, or a divine thunderclap of inspiration. It's not a single perfect concept that lands, fully formed, in your head, but a series of developing connections that progress over time to form a coherent structure. In his book *Where Good Ideas Come From*, Steven Johnson describes ideas as networks of neurons firing in synch with each other inside your brain: A new idea is a new configuration that has never been formed before, the component parts evolving and developing as they connect and expand. He calls this the 'Slow Hunch' and suggests a good idea often has a lengthy incubation period. He uses the example of Charles Darwin who was unknowingly sketching out early iterations of his Theory of Evolution years before he actually formed the whole idea consciously.

In late middle age Mark Rothko, who'd begun his artistic life as a figurative painter, created those famous vast canvasses of deep red for the Seagram Building. A wag journalist at the time, unimpressed on seeing these simplistic, almost child-like blobs of colour asked him how long it had taken him to paint. Rothko's answer? 'Fifty four years'.

The means by which we make art are never wholly conscious. You're going on intuition: you're reaching into your unconscious, contacting stored or repressed memories. When we were casting my play *The Holy Rosenbergs*, the actor Philip Arditti, a talented performer with great instincts himself, came in to meet the director Laurie Sansom and me for the part of Simon, the Rabbi. On my way in to auditions that morning I ran into him at the coffee place in the National's foyer and found him studying the play. I sat down briefly to thank him for coming in and he said something that startled me. He pointed out that he had initially found the first line of the play, a line belonging to the Rabbi, curiously mundane. The line is this:

Rabbi   Are those pillars new?

My first instinct was to panic. 'What have I done?' I thought. 'He's right, of course he's right, it's a ridiculous line. Why did I do that? I'm a total fraud. The play is absurd. What on earth was Nick Hytner thinking programming it, had he completely taken leave of his senses?!'

Philip went on, though, to say that, as he began to understand what was going on, he realised the purpose of the line. 'Oh', I bluffed, 'yes, good. Thank you for noticing'. Probably sensing my confusion, he patiently explained that the existence of the pillars indicates something very disturbing. The story of the play begins the day before North London kosher caterers David and Lesley Rosenberg are due to bury their eldest son. Simon is the local Rabbi and knows the family and their home intimately. In fact he almost certainly walks past the house on a daily basis so he knows there aren't usually pillars on the porch. So when he asks 'are those pillars new', he's implying that they've been erected *since* the son's death. A few lines later we learn from the youngest son Jonny that 'Dad put them up himself' confirming that the father is acting irrationally and manically and is clearly on the edge of some sort of breakdown. Who would start erecting pillars in front of the house immediately on learning of their son's death in war? Of course, we don't act rationally at these moments, and my instinct was that David, the father, would transfer his pain and guilt with furious and constant activity. The Rabbi's signalling to this means the play has tension from the very first line.

Looking at it now all these years later, I wonder how conscious I was when I was writing it. You write in a sort of elsewhere. Half present. The pillars I had in my mind's eye were very specific. My own father had had some built in front of the house I grew up in. I don't remember when they went up, I just remember there was a time when they weren't there and a time when they were, they sort of emerged into my consciousness. Re-reading that first scene for this book I unearthed more symbolism in the pillars. Jonny's damning indictment of them as 'Chav Palace' suggests the presence of a cultural and spiritual gulf between the generations even at a time of terrible grief. A fault-line runs through this family that might never be repaired. This is not lost on the Rabbi who, in a clumsy attempt to lighten the mood, asks: 'They're not holding the house up then?' Much later, as the play comes to a close that same night, Jonny, in a frenzy of anger and expiation, attacks the pillars with an axe.

The Holy Rosenbergs was written quickly, in a sort of fever. It had to be. It was an instinctive response to the increasingly polarised conversations I was hearing all around me – and having myself – about Israel and Palestine, about identity and justice, about tribal loyalty and personal responsibility. It had to be as raw a reaction to that intractable situation as possible or it would have been tainted with prevarication and compromise. It was supposed to make people angry on both sides of the fence and it did. 'You won't make any friends with this play', I was told. But anything else, to me, would have felt disingenuous and pointless. As I wrote I was making connections with my background, my upbringing and my Jewish heritage that were both conscious and unconscious.

'I've always felt like a middleman', Neil Simon said, 'like the typist. Somebody somewhere is saying: "this is what they say now, this is what they say next".' Simon talks of having a tiny typist living inside his head, working away day and night while Big Neil is relaxing or reading or eating or listening to music. When he can access that tiny typist and let them do their work he knows he's on to something. Paul Klee described drawing as 'taking a line for a walk', suggesting that art may begin with a conscious impulse, but at some point the unconscious has to be allowed to take over. But how on earth do you *consciously* begin to try to access the *unc*onscious?

You often hear, when people discuss the writing process, about the terror of the blank page. It's as if beginning to write is opening a door onto an endless, barren wasteland. And into this vast expanse of nothingness we're meant to wade waist deep without any kind of navigational aid. But, if you think about it, that's not actually the case. Think back to that five-year-old. Our minds are full of patterns and structures we could use to steer us through this unmapped territory. Even in adulthood our brains are constantly whirring, constantly processing data and emotions. Our memories are crammed with experiences and people and stories and ideas. What we really need when we're writing drama is singularity. Focus. Clarity. It's not the blankness of the imaginary page that should alarm us, but the density of it. It's that page with no space left, every spare patch filled, scrawled over: words upon words, thoughts lost inside thoughts: that's the page you should be petrified of. The page so overwhelmed by a forest of ink it resembles one of those Rothko paintings. When there are too many options it's harder to focus, and this lack of focus can be fatal in locating your idea and following its logical thread. If your mind is haywire with the ideas you've had and the characters you've conjured and the adventures you want them to go on and all of it noisily competing for supremacy, how can you see where the play is going?

So instead of desperately marking a blank page, there should, conversely, be a process of mental sweeping up, of what Peter Brook in his book *The Empty Space* describes as *weeding the garden*: all creative art being a process of *elimination*. When I was a post-graduate student I directed my first play *The Sins of Dalia Baumgarten* in a fringe space called The Etcetera Theatre, which was a room above a pub in Camden. My directing teacher, the magnificently irreverent Annie Castledine, came to watch an early rehearsal. She sat expressionless, puffing on cigarettes, as we presented to her a run of the play where I had the actors frenziedly tackling all the complexities and contradictions of their characters and their journeys. Afterwards she commanded we go to Joe Allen's, the Covent Garden basement brassiere, for dinner to discuss the play. After dinner she sat back, lit yet another cigarette, and fixed me with a hard and disconcerting stare. Finally she said in her rasping Sheffield accent and through a blizzard of smoke: 'only give the actors *one* thing to want at a time, love. Don't confuse the dears'.

In about a mile radius of my house there's a smattering of cafés with large tables and sympathetic (or even better apathetic) staff, where I can set up my shop and write. These places are usually buzzing, but not hectic, and with the kind of austere, distressed furniture that prevents too much luxuriating. A silent, solitary room of my own is useless to me. The idea of being completely alone with only a desk and my naked thoughts makes me want to tear the skin off my face. I need people, I need noise, I need to have the rattle and prattle of voices and machinery and cutlery and crockery, people coming and going, or chatting and eating, the current of life. I need something to tune out so I can zone in on my objective: To remove the clutter of my mind and access the unconscious.

The Grand Café still stands on the site where the first coffee house opened for business in Oxford in 1650 by a man called Jacob, the son of Jewish immigrants. Since then coffee houses have proliferated across Britain and played a pivotal role in the great flowering of intellectual thought known as the Enlightenment. The average Brit's daily refreshment changed from booze to caffeine (the water being full of disease) so productivity and innovation soared. It was also, as Steven Johnson points out, a place where people from all different backgrounds and fields of expertise congregated, shared their knowledge, debated and discussed, the kind of place where, to paraphrase Matt Ridley, *ideas came to have sex.*

It's a Wednesday morning and there's a gentle hum in the café I've stumbled into. It's not busy. A few customers are dotted about, laptops agape. I open mine and stare at it. I hear the hiss of the coffee machine sputtering into life and I try to encourage my brain to do the same. I notice ruefully the other lap-toppers are deeply engrossed in their work, their eyes shining with purpose. It's no wonder. Before they'd even reach the café, the walk they took released endorphins and proteins such as Brain Derived Neurotrophic Factor (BDNF) that improve cognitive function.

This morning, though, my BDNF has gone for his own coffee break. I gaze about, my mind bleary, my cognitive function taking its sweet time to power up. It's still early and the waiting-staff are unrushed. A young woman wearing what my mother would describe as an 'interesting combination' approaches with a menu clipped to a small rectangular board. She speaks to me, but I don't hear what she says, because I'm already lost in my thoughts. I've begun, without noticing, to sink into that elsewhere, to retreat from the real world. When we write we exist in a liminal state, in a sort of future conditional tense. It's a strange paradox that the playwright lives so often detached from the present moment, and yet is charged with conjuring characters who feel alive, who feel utterly present.

Luigi Pirandello believed that his characters 'spoke to him'. These disembodied voices, he thought, had agency separate from his control. 'No-one can know better than yourself', they told him, 'that we are living beings, more alive than those who breathe and dress; perhaps we are less real, but we are certainly *more true*' (my italics). Harold Pinter wrote: 'characters … possess a momentum of their own my job is not to impose on them … The relationship between author and characters is a highly respectful one, both ways.' That active negative is striking here. 'My job is *not* to impose'. Pinter and Pirandello seem to be implying that the process of making a play is a sort of freedom *from* writing. The writer must be confident enough to let the characters point the way, to take on a life of their own, or, as Pinter put it to allow 'them to carry their own can by giving them legitimate elbow room'.

'Anything to eat?' What's this, what's happening, who said that? Oh it's, yes, I remember, I'm … Oh God I'm giving her that witless look. She's twisting her neck slightly, her eyes narrowing. I look at her. I suppose I should speak here. I should, at the very least, acknowledge her presence, but I still I haven't surfaced from the seabed of my thoughts. I open my mouth but it's as inactive as the gagging laptop. It's like I'm inside the drum of a washing machine, the outside world muffled and remote.

I'm rooting around in the basement of the ideas shop in my brain. I'm reaching for the idea that will spark off this book. The one you're reading now. By the time I finish up in the café I'll have sketched out a basic structure. Three parts, like a three-act play, beginning with how we start to write, what ideas are and how we use them. (The keen-eyed among you will notice there's a fourth part to this book, which I began as we were heading into lockdown and felt it necessary to adapt my structure as the world altered irrevocably around me.) In the second 'act', I'd write about the technical specifics: how to build a structure, how to create tension and conflict, how to write character, what is a reversal, how do we resolve our play and what happens to it when it's actually up and running. I'll pepper this chapter, I thought, with writing exercises and practical advice and theatre anecdotes. Finally, I would end on some thoughts about the writer's 'voice'. I knew I wanted it to be a personal book. It's all I have to give. My experience. Dramatic instinct isn't something that can really be taught, but I have *done* it. I've written plays and had them on. I've sallied forth on that journey, I've made a life as a playwright and taken the beatings in the process, I've got the scars and the emotional contusions to prove it and I can report back from that undiscovered country, I believe, with some authority.

'Oh. Uh. Nothing. Thanks', I find myself saying finally like a drunk staggering home, the internal GPS kicking in. This absence is a common state for me because writing is an effort that requires both right and left brain to be firing on all cylinders simultaneously. You're trying to access the unconscious and apply your craft at the same time.

When I was starting out at as a young, bushy-eyed, bright-tailed playwright at the NT Studio clutching my desperately earnest early attempt at dramatic immortality, I was given a mentor. This was a writer, not much older than I, called Simon Block (now a highly esteemed screenwriter with films like *The Eichmann Show* and *The Windermere Children* under his belt). At that stage in his career he'd already written a couple of crackling, blackly comic plays like *Chimps* about door-to-door salesmen for Hampstead Theatre and *Not a Game for Boys* about three viciously competitive, amateur table tennis players for the Royal Court. He lived not far from me in Barnet in North London, so Jack Bradley, the National's literary manager, thought that would grease the wheels of our relationship. 'We call him the Finchley Mamet', Bradley chortled darkly as he wrote down Simon's address. That didn't reassure me. Still, I sent over my pages and he called and arranged to meet. Anxiously, I arrived at Café Rouge, a faux French bistro all blood reds and wicker situated in a vast, soulless cinema complex off the busy North Circular. Simon was already there swathed in his coat, collar turned up, a tall glass of un-drunk coca cola on the table in front of him. 'Yeah, I read your pages', he said gnomically, his eyes drifting up to the heavens. He was fiddling with a small pink sachet, tumescent with fake sugar, tapping it with his fingers. My breath stopped. I tried to read his expression, but he was lost in thought, reaching for the precise words. After a long silence he opened his mouth to speak, but instead, suddenly, ripped open the sachet and poured the synthetic sugar into the coke. Jesus, I thought, this guy's a maniac. 'Um', I started, 'Isn't that stuff already loaded with sugar?' 'I like', he said, the slyest of grins cutting across his face, 'the way it fizzes.' I began looking for the exit. Perhaps I could just leg it and never mention this to anyone again. 'So your play', he said suddenly stirring his cocktail, 'yeah, ok, you can do dialogue, you can do character', I nodded, thinking, sounds like there's a 'but' coming here. 'But', he said, and then he sighed, looked up to the heavens again. He took a sip of his drink and then said something that has stayed with me ever since: 'But why am I watching *these* characters and not their next door neighbours?'

Beckett believed that *form* should place *content* under pressure. It's not enough to put characters on a stage doing and saying things, however interesting those things might be, there must a metaphorical context within which the action takes place, and which reveals a truth about our shared human condition. The vital simplicity of two querulous tramps waiting by a leafless tree for a character that never comes is, at once, supremely clear and utterly devastating. What Simon Block was telling me was that a play is a metaphor. The ideas we use to write them must have a complex molecular structure.

Now, every time I come to write, I ask myself the same question: why are we watching these people and not other people? Within what context are we watching them behave, and what about that behaviour makes their story dramatically compelling? When I came to write *What We Did To Weinstein*, I wanted to put the audience inside the memories of Josh, a young British Jew who is traumatised by his childhood and joins the Israeli Army in order to find his identity. Under arrest for breaking ranks and releasing a terrorist suspect, he is interrogated about his motives. This catapults him into recollections of a time when he returned home to London to remonstrate with his dying father. This echoing structure allowed me to move easily between time and place, from, for example, the West Bank in 2001 one instant, to North London in 1995 the next. This jagged chronology could then reveal the fractured nature of Josh's mind as well as unravel the citric shards of conflict between characters so closely connected yet so polarised by this particular political issue. With *The Holy Rosenbergs* I showed another family being torn apart by their polarised positions on the same issue. When the son dies in an air-battle over Gaza and the sister joins a human rights commission to investigate war crimes in that same conflict, the family members are forced to find common ground in order to collectively mourn. In *Filthy Business*, the rubber shop at the centre of the story became a metaphor for the safe haven sought by Yetta as a refugee from persecution. The conflict comes when the rest of the family have competing visions about how to run it.

There's an old saying that having a second child isn't doubling the workload it's multiplying it by a thousand. The sudden addition of a sibling, a *rival*, creates a multitude of unforeseen conflicts. It's the same with plays. When characters are placed in a confined space with their opposites, the sparks will fly.

So some external force or setting or structure must be found to focus the characters emotionally or psychologically and add heat to the action. Take Harold Pinter's *Betrayal*. What's the idea at the heart of this play? If your answer goes something like: 'it's a semi-autobiographical examination of the inner workings of an affair', or, 'it's a dark comedy with stilted dialogue about sexual infidelity among the literati' you're only half right. What turns Pinter's subject into 'an idea' is that he chooses to tell the story backwards. Chronologically, the beginning is the end and the end the beginning. The peeling away of time mirrors the peeling away of the characters' identity and integrity as they deceive each other and themselves. Structure reveals theme. Or to put it another way the story *is* the way it's told, as much as it is the events that happen within it.

Roy Williams's *Sing Yer Heart Out For the Lads* runs chronologically but also connects a specific time constraint to the themes it's trying to explore. In this case, themes of nationalism and belonging. Here, the action in a South London pub plays out in parallel with a football match between England and, naturally, Germany, where England, naturally, lose. As England's fortunes decline, so does the behaviour of the characters. Interweaving theme, setting, character and time constraint, Williams reveals how, given the right circumstances, repressed bitterness can quickly turn to open hostility and racism.

But it doesn't have to be time constraint that determines the form and completes the idea. For her play *Welcome to Thebes*, Moira Buffini threw together several of the great dynastic Greek mythological characters into a contemporary, war-torn African republic. She was able to ingeniously interweave Antigone, Eurydice and Creon, Hippolytus, Phaedra and Theseus, and Dionysus and bring their ancient stories crashing into the twenty-first century to explore some enduring truths about human nature and political hierarchies.

Frank McGuinness's *Someone Who'll Watch Over Me* places three hostages, an American, an Irishman and an Englishman, in a cell somewhere in Lebanon and gradually tightens the screws. In this setting McGuinness is able to put national idiosyncrasies and tensions under the microscope. Prisons can be psychological as well as concrete, as in Florian Zeller's play *The Father*, which explores the world of a dementia sufferer completely through his eyes. It's a deceivingly elegant piece of theatre that quickly discombobulates us so that we empathise with the protagonist. In Scene One we're introduced to his daughter in an awkward but naturalistic scene, but in Scene Two a completely different actor enters, breezily and without fanfare, claiming to be that *same* daughter. It places you inside the disintegrating mind of the main character and, in doing so, captures the terrifying, treacherous nature of his shattered reality. *Form must put content under pressure.*

Dennis Kelly's *Taking Care of Baby* uses the tropes of verbatim theatre to draw us into a story about injustice and child death: about the nature of truth, scientific authority and artistic authenticity. I saw Anthony Clark's production in a very early preview at Hampstead Theatre knowing nothing about it. At that time in the British Theatre there was a penchant for verbatim work, which matched the audience's hunger for journalistic authenticity. Kelly ran with this idea, even putting 'himself' in the play as a disembodied interviewer, the playwright, interacting with the characters in his drama. He created a world so completely believable I'm certain by the end of the first half most of the audience was convinced they were already familiar with the story. They weren't. He'd totally made it up. I was taken in utterly and I remember asking the director at the interval why he would commission a verbatim play from a writer as imaginative as Dennis Kelly. He smiled impishly and said 'ask me that question again after the second half'. In that second half, the play begins to chip away at your sense of reality, forces you to question the veracity of the information we receive, question the nature of reported 'facts' by fragmenting the narrative. This 'verbatim' style allowed those themes to be revealed.

A few years ago I was asked to lead a course in How to Begin Play-Writing at the National Theatre. I agreed only on the condition that I explain to everyone up front that there's no roadmap for writing a good play, I can't hand out a formula for success. What I could do is talk about my own experience as a practising playwright. I realised I could talk about the mistakes I've made in my writing as well as the things I've got right. I've failed as much, if not more, than I've succeeded and learned more from the failures than the successes. I've enjoyed what might generously be described as an eclectic career. Looked at from the outside it probably appears wildly inconsistent. This wasn't planned, but I also didn't avoid it. I was twenty-six when my play *Happy Savages* was professionally produced at the Hammersmith Lyric Studio. While it was playing, a highly renowned director cautioned me not to be drawn into the more lucrative and 'less credible' area of series television work. (Times have changed.) I didn't listen. I wanted to make my living from writing and I was willing to do whatever it took. I've written gloriously trashy soaps and serious drama documentary. I've written tons of radio drama, from adapting a comedy thriller to an experimentally esoteric devised piece about love in London. I've written a modern reworking of Aristophanes and an afternoon play about teaching English during the Afghan war.

In the theatre I recently alarmed some people by turning in a light romantic comedy after developing a reputation for work that tackled themes of tribal identity, religious war, nuclear proliferation and Holocaust denial. But however varied the subject matter, the actual day-to-day job of writing drama never feels radically different. I call on a broadly similar set of skills and techniques. Whether it's *Games For Lovers* at the Vaults or *Our Class* at the National I'm ultimately interested in creating living action: trying to communicate the human condition through characters in conflict. How I do that is what I'm going to explore in this next chapter.

2 Story

1 Structure

After grinding the beans, she pours cold milk into a metal steaming pitcher, about a third full. She takes the steam wand and pumps it a couple of times to clear out any residual liquid, then dips the tip of the wand into the milk and fires up the jet. As the foam rises and the milk swells she gradually lowers the pitcher into the milk, the tip always submerged and tilted to create a vortex. When the milk reaches a temperature of about sixty-five degrees and its volume doubles, she shuts off the steam. She taps the base of the pitcher hard on the countertop. One. Two. Three. This compresses the foam. She pours a shot of espresso into a large cup and then pours the foamed milk into that, aiming for the centre and spiralling out progressively toward the rim of the cup until it's brimming with froth and the cappuccino is ready.

This process will forever be a thing of beauty to me. I'm an avid coffee drinker, and, if you've had as many cappuccinos as I have, you know each barista has their own distinctive touch. It's true, however, if they don't follow a formula, if they just make it up as they go along, they're probably not going to end up with a cappuccino.

I remember one winter in my twenties moving into a new flat and having some shady guys lay down laminate flooring on the cheap. Laminate floors are a layer cake of synthetic materials with a photograph of wood grain glued to the surface. When spring came and the temperature rose, the 'wood' expanded in the heat and large swollen bubbles of air appeared all over the floor lifting it up in unseemly blotches. A man called John, who worked in my dad's shop, came over to the flat with his toolbox. 'He can fix anything, John', my Dad always told me. John took one look at the bubbly floor, shook his head gravely and said. 'It can't breathe.' He said nothing else. He took a Stanley knife from his box, knelt down and cut out a small section of the material along each wall. Suddenly able to expand and contract, the bubbling abated and the floor sat there for the duration performing its singular purpose – that of being a flat and even surface to walk on. Sometimes there's no substitute for basic common sense.

During my time writing series television I discovered each show has its own handbook called 'a bible'. This bible lays out, in detail, the fundamental components of the show: the feel of it, the precinct in which the action takes place, the biography of the principle characters involved and how each episode tends to be formatted. It also says a lot about the dramatic structure of an episode. A crime drama, for example, might open with the discovery of a dead body, the Hazmat team sterilising the crime scene, the maverick cop arriving, sniffing out hunches, then wearing out his shoe leather going door to door, breaking protocol even as the boss tries to rein him in and make him do things by the book. Further complications are introduced and the body count piles up, putting pressure to the cop and his jobs-worth superior, but still he persists in doing things 'his way' until a flash of inspiration or a lucky coincidence in the final act leads him to fit the last piece to the jigsaw puzzle and trap the killer. At the start of each new series a sub-bible would be created laying out where that season was going, what might happen to the characters next, and what the general tenor was to be. Some shows are more specific than others, but essentially each reveals a sort of house style. You know the world you're in. You know the genre.

In the age of streaming, TV drama has been forced to stretch itself. In an ever-crowded market some TV drama has had to break out of the hyper-formulaic, even to be ground-breaking and experimental. Great television has always been capable of reinventing the rules as well as any art form – just look at *Edge of Darkness* or *Mad Men* or *The Singing Detective* or *The Garry Shandling Show* or *I May Destroy You* – but it still has to obey the strictures of the medium. It's also a broadly collaborative process from the very start. Even if there's a single writer, there are producers and script editors and commissioning editors, all contributing to the feel and architecture of the programme: and that's before you put pen to paper, or finger to keyboard.

When it comes to plays, though, there's no bible. There are no genres and no formulas, there's just you and your imagination. You alone in that overgrown word garden you now have to weed and cultivate. Each new play has to find its own structure and style. The characters are unique to a single narrative and the play lasts for as long as it needs to, to tell the story. The theatre is freed from the literal imperative of the screen, and can exist somewhere in space and time simply by implanting the suggestion of a place in the audience's mind. 'Think', Shakespeare writes in his prologue to *Henry V*, 'when we talk of horses that you see them'. An actor could walk on to a bare stage and declare 'We are now on the moon', and the audience would suspend its disbelief. On screen, if we don't see the craters and the space suits, *we're not on the moon*. Genre is not something the playwright often considers, because theatre itself is the genre. When it comes to writing a play, all these components – shape, character, texture, conflict, space and time – have to evolve naturally and simultaneously out of the same initial complex idea.

If theatre is the genre, a play *is* its structure. What that structure is becomes a fundamental question of creative invention. Pinter said that when he wrote he kept his 'nose to the ground'. By which I think he meant he was truffling out the play's *true* construction hidden within the story his characters were trying to tell. His job was to follow his instincts. Alan Ayckbourn wrote that it 'really isn't a choice I consciously make. I certainly don't decide when I sit down to write: today I'm going to write a comedy.'

'I'm not really that interested in genre', says Annie Baker, the American author of brilliantly esoteric plays like *John* and *The Flick* and *Circle, Mirror, Transformation.* 'I guess it goes back to my resistance to rules and conventions.' In her play *The Antipodes* the characters remain trapped in a single room trying to invent a 'monster story', but their imagination darts all over the place. The play wafts and wends along, characters tell personal stories, shaggy dog stories, losing their virginity stories, fantasy stories, ghost stories, fairy stories: they ruminate on the nature of story itself and finally fall through an intellectual worm hole and wonder if there are, indeed, any stories left to tell. 'If people say my plays span or incorporate different genres', Baker says, 'I hope that just means they're surprising.' This is because, like Pinter and Ayckbourn, she too follows her nose. 'If you're making a choice from fear or obedience', Baker says, 'it's the wrong choice'.

But there has to be some conscious application of craft involved in writing our plays. The question is how we marry our unique instincts to some essential structure that will be the dramatic mechanism by which we can communicate our ideas.

EXERCISE 1: Take a beloved fairy-tale like Cinderella, Hansel and Gretel or Sleeping Beauty and deconstruct it. Take it apart bit by bit. Look at how it works. What is the set up, who are the central characters, what do they want? What happens and how do they run into complications and conflicts? What dilemma is the character presented with, what realisation do they come to and how is it resolved? Once you've deconstructed it, put it back together this time with a new spin. How would you do it? Where would you set it and when? What would the style of the piece be, how would the dialogue sound, what tempos and rhythms would they follow?

The variations are limitless, but the concept remains the same. A new text is built on the foundations of a classic structure. Having that secure foundation can allow you to base-jump into something very personal. It can access your distinctive voice or style without self-consciousness, and it can even allow you to reinvent the form itself.

Stage writing has to be this layered, because, in order to work, it has to have a special sort of sturdiness. Unlike prose writers or screenwriters the playwright's words have to travel across a physical distance, across space and time. A divide must be crossed. Our words have to leave the playing area, reach across the stalls and ripple out to the far corners of the theatre. I think this physical quality is why plays stay with us long after the curtain has fallen. How you achieve this is what I'm going to explore in the next section.

2 Distance

This is how Pinter's *Betrayal* begins. A woman, Emma, is sitting at a corner table. A man, Jerry, approaches with drinks. He sits. They smile, toast each other and drink. Jerry sits back and looks at her. Finally he says: 'Well . . .'

Doesn't seem like much does it? But hidden in the ambiguity is a challenge. 'Well', isn't written as a question, but as a statement: and the ellipses, the tail of dots on the end of the word, suggest there's more Jerry wants to say, but, for whatever reason, doesn't. So a line that at first appears innocuous, especially for an opening gambit, on closer inspection, becomes more dynamic. Isolate it in your mind for a moment and you'll recognise it for what it is: a subtle act of aggression, of belligerence: a sly incursion into the psychic territory of the person he's addressing. Dare, Jerry seems to be saying to Emma, to fill in the gap. And that act of incitement prompts us to lean forward, to imperceptibly hold our breath and listen, listen with a quality that's more intense, because, before we've even noticed it, a distance has opened up: a distance between what is being said and what is being felt. And in that distance a tension has been created. And that's how to write dialogue for the theatre.

Pinter notoriously began many of his early plays with no dialogue at all, with a prolonged period of silence. It's a sort of mute overture to presage a journey into the unknowable. A mood is created, the atmospheric pressure increased.

Let's see what happens next.

Emma appears to take the bait and takes a tentative step into the snake pit. 'How are you?' she asks. You sense immediately her hand has been forced, or that there is some other, deeper question she wants to ask, but doesn't.

Jerry answers. 'All right', he says. But we quickly discover this is a direct untruth, because only a line later, after she says 'you look well' he responds by saying 'I'm *not* well actually' (my italics).

What I mean to demonstrate by examining this small section in such obsessively forensic detail is that, to write something dramatically taut, every line must be infused with some oppositional attitude. Pinter has here a seemingly contradictory ability to be at once playful and sinister and it gives the writing its tang. I'm not advising you to copy this style – that could only end in parody, which, in the theatre, is fatal – but it's worth taking a moment here to look at what makes Pinter's stage writing so effective. According to him he was trying to find a language where 'under what is being said, another thing is being said'. A friction has been created. Two sticks are being rubbed together to create a spark, and that static ripples out across the stage and into the audience. It travels. When there is no friction between word and meaning, it droops.

In soaps you often find characters telling each other things they obviously already know. You'll often hear dialogue along the lines of 'You can't talk to me like that, I'm your mother.' Or 'Behave, you just got out of prison, you wanna go back?' No distance is travelled here because no subtext exists underneath the words. I wrote a stack of soaps in my twenties and thirties so I know there's a reason for this over-explaining, that there's method in the madness. With such a ravenous appetite for story and such a high volume of incident, it can be a nifty technique to keep the audience updated if they miss a few episodes. A character will remind another they had an affair with so and so, or they're in trouble with such and such and it loops us back into the plot. A highly skilled and experienced soap writer will surreptitiously slip in a little helpful information to the dialogue to give the viewer useful context to the next dramatic moments. The characters know this stuff already, the information's for the audience, because the relationship between the audience and the soap is of a different nature to the one an audience has with a play.

In a drama the story has an end. A character has an arc, a curving, finite trajectory that climbs, peaks and descends, coming to land at some critical point. The audience is pre-programmed to understand this when they set out. They know, though they don't know how, that this story they're watching will conclude in some way. They hope that this conclusion will be cathartic. That fact that it ends is a cleansing. In soaps, which have come to be daintily known as 'continuing dramas', the story as *no* end. The characters' journeys are like marks on an endless electrocardiogram: high spikes, low troughs, flat-lining then starting all over again in a random sequence. This works in episodic story telling, but it severely limits character development so there is no catharsis. There is no soul cleansing because there is no conclusion.

What soaps do have in common with great drama is the regular deployment of tragic irony. Often a character is desperate to break out of their current situation and make a 'fresh start', but can't, either because of their own failings, or because of some outside influence they're unaware of. *We* intuit this trap, invisible to the character, and so we feel pity for them.

Sometimes we're even in possession of a vital piece of information that the character isn't. That means we see their destiny far clearer than they do. This time there's a distance between what the character *thinks* is the case and what we *know* to be the case. There's a scene in *Betrayal* where Jerry assumes Robert has only very recently discovered about the affair he's having with Emma. Emma is Robert's wife. Jerry expects their conversation to go in a certain direction. We, however, know that Robert has known about this affair for years. We watch Jerry's flailing confusion from the edge of our seats. When the truth is revealed it is Jerry who suddenly feels the victim of betrayal. The rug has been pulled from under him.

In a memorable episode of *EastEnders*, Carol Jackson, heavily pregnant with the child of her new partner Dan, suspects that Dan has been having an affair with her teenage daughter Bianca. We know this to be true, because we've seen them at it. We are in possession of information Carol isn't. So we watch in tense anticipation as she, tearful, desperate, vibrating with anger, confronts Dan about the affair. When he flatly denies it, she takes his hand and places it on her distended stomach. 'Swear on the baby's life', she demands. It's an electric moment because we know that, in a moral universe, whatever Dan does next must surely have terrible consequences. If he tells her the truth there will be an explosive row, and if he doesn't, he will be guilty of a shameful lie and will have consciously cursed his unborn child. Dan places his hand on Carol's stomach and, on the child's life, swears his innocence. It's a jaw-dropping moment, febrile with anticipation because a series of expectations have now been placed in our minds about what will happen next.

A similar scenario plays out in John Osborne's *Look Back in Anger*, when Jimmy, unaware as we are that Alison is pregnant, rages at her, 'If only you could have a child and it would die ... if only I could watch you face that'. King Lear is forever cursing his children's unborn progeny, incensed at their ingratitude. We know, because it's hard-wired into us by story after story, that Dan's crime cannot possibly go unpunished. And, as with *Betrayal*, we spend the rest of the time waiting for the bomb to go off and the terrible truth to be revealed.

EXERCISE 2: Write a scene, a two hander, two characters 'A' and 'B'. 'A' has something 'B' desperately wants, but can't give it to 'B' and can't tell 'B' why. A crude example would be this: Two people in a desert. 'A' has a flask of water, but it's poisoned because he intends to assassinate a third, off-stage, character, 'C'. 'B' can't know that, but is dying of thirst and wants to drink the tainted water. Conflict ensues and, ideally, sparks are lit. The scene doesn't have to come to any clever conclusion, it can start and end at any point: the characters can be any age, gender, profession, it can be set in any place, in any time period.

When I've asked people in my writing workshops to attempt this exercise, their scenarios are invariably more interesting than my example above. Their scenes fly off the page, they're full of originality, conflict, humour and tension. Because the characters have such direct and immediate *wants*, their dialogue is active and taut rather than winding and vague. It works dramatically because a character has been given a desire, a *want* and that *want* necessarily mutates from a *thought* into an *action*. When two opposing *want-actions* come together that turns into a *conflict*.

In my crude scenario, character B wants the water in character A's flask. So B's action is that she '*tries to get the water*'. Character A, however, wants to preserve the liquid in his flask, so his action, '*stopping B from getting the water*' is in direct *conflict* with the action of B '*getting the water*'. The competing actions create the dramatic tension. The audience 'cares' because we tend to *connect* with characters that *want* something very badly, try to *get* it, and find themselves blocked.

But, in order to take flight, the intensity of the action always has to be leavened with a kind of cool detachment in the delivery. The events in Tadeusz Slobodzianek's play *Our Class* are deeply distressing. The narrative follows a class of ten children through the horrors of segregation, war and genocide. But while I was adapting the text for the English production at the NT, whenever I allowed the language to become too emotive the play jarred. Counter-intuitively, the heaviness and richness of the material demanded a ruthless austerity. It required a restraint that appeared to work in direct opposition to the feral violence of the action. The same was true in performance. A lot of the story is delivered by 'direct address', a character speaking directly to the audience. When the actors put too much heat under the text the delivery fell flat. It was alienating. The play only began to fly when there was a contradiction or a *distance* between what was being said and how it was being played. Take this speech spoken by a young and naïve Rysiek.

> **Rysiek**   They grabbed me and threw me to the floor. They snatched my cap off my head and stuffed it in my mouth. One man sat on my legs, while another grabbed my head. I saw a third man reach behind a stove and pull out this cudgel. I bit down on my cap, ready for it. He beat me, and beat me, and beat me ... I chewed my cap to shreds. Then they sat me on this stool by a wall. They got a good grip of my hair and smashed my head against the wall ... over and over ... so hard I thought my skull would shatter. After that they yanked out great clumps of hair. All the time they were repeating ... Confess. Give us the names of your accomplices. I knew if I talked, the others'd get the same treatment. Better to take the punishment on my own. I didn't know a man could take so much.

The character is reliving his torture moment by moment, it's almost unbearable, but the delivery required the actor to be disinterested. Distanced. The actor had to separate from the action in order to make us feel the power of it. All the actors in the production, though deeply invested in their characters and their stories after weeks of immersing themselves in this blood-soaked period of history, realised they had to find a way of delivering these heavyweight monologues as weightlessly as possible. It was the only way the words could be successfully carried across the stage to the audience and penetrate deep into its conscience.

The act of making theatre is the act of embracing these contradictions because theatre is such an acutely human activity. During rehearsals of *Our Class* one of the many things we studied was Claude Lanzmann's seminal 1985 Holocaust documentary, *Shoah*. There's a remarkable section where Lanzmann interviews a survivor whose extraordinary testimony of the barbarism that was visited on him is memorably compelling due to a broad smile that cuts across his face. 'Why do you smile all the time?' asks Lanzmann. We humans are contradictory, complex creatures. It's how we negotiate this savage, irrational world.

3 Character

Tennessee Williams wrote this: 'I think of writing as something more organic than words, something closer to *being* and *action*. I want to work more and more with a more *plastic* theatre ...'(my italics).

As we've seen, if a distance is to be travelled a tension must be embedded into the text: a contradiction between what is being said and what is being meant. As a general rule, the greater that distance the further the words will travel, but this *plasticity* means writing for the theatre can be a slippery business.

Williams writes about fragile people full of passion yet unable to emotionally connect. In his essay *Person To Person* he explains his work in terms of catching and holding the audience's attention. 'I have never doubted', he writes, 'there are people – millions! – to say things to. We come to each other gradually, but with love.' This need to connect makes the business of writing for the stage not only slippery, but incredibly raw. Like all human enterprises it can be wracked with flaws and supremely disappointing, but also uniquely moving.

I've always preferred writing the first draft of a play freehand, pen on paper. I want to feel the nib touching the pad, moving across it. I feel the writing has a different quality because of it. I can't prove that, but I do know from experience how exposed you are when you write for the stage. There's nowhere to hide. Use all the software you like, employ all the bells and whistles when producing it, but the success or failure of your play will always come down to this formulation: actors delivering words you made up to an audience.

Before the actors can do this they'll want to know four cardinal things: What does my character want? How do they go about getting it? What is their status in the world of the play? Who are they at their core?

My first car when I was seventeen was a second-hand electric blue Suzuki jeep. It looked snazzy but was scarily flimsy of frame, rickety and rattling in the wind. A strong gust would send the thing tilting off its wheels, almost toppling over: it was a harrowing ordeal to drive it in a storm. The spare wheel of a Suzuki is classically bracketed to the back of the jeep, the canvas cover of the wheel normally displaying a geometric silhouette of an African rhino, white on black. The original owner, a friend of my father's and a bit of a joker, had customised this wheel cover by adding a second rhino amorously mounting the first. I now realise this might explain why, in those days, I was constantly being pulled over by the police.

I was even more naïve back then and barely conscious of this offensive display I was brazenly parading around North West London. In those days I was an awkward, bone-thin boy with a dense mop of straw-straight hair and a terror of the opposite sex. I once drove my friend Guy to a house party in Edgware and my blue jeep impressed two of the most staggeringly beautiful women I'd ever seen. Guy, always more front-footed than I, though equally socially hapless, invited them for a spin. The police officers who pulled us over that night approached with a swaggering resentment. What on earth must they have thought? Two young women hung out the back window of a garishly painted flash-wagon careening in the wind and with rhino-porn on its spare wheel. What cock-sure stallion did they expect to find in the driver's seat? When they encountered me, this diffident, willowy geek, they must have been utterly bemused. To see a glimpse of a person is not to see them at all.

When I had to present myself at the local police station for my 'producer' – you had to show physical evidence, updated insurance documents, driver's licence etc. – a young man with darkish skin came in, slightly breathless. He was concerned about a missing friend. The desk sergeant, who'd been cool but courteous with me, suddenly flipped. He changed his attitude radically becoming aggressive and brusque with the man, overtly intimidating and suspicious. It was shocking to me. The man seemed to take it in his stride, upset but unsurprised. He stayed calm but quietly persisted, standing his ground. To my amazement, the desk sergeant then, collusively, rolled his eyes at *me*. I remember thinking 'why's he rolling his eyes at me? I'm the felon!'

Thirty years on a *Liberty Investigates* study revealed that, during the coronavirus pandemic in the UK, black, Asian and minority ethnic people were 54 per cent more likely to be fined for breaking the lockdown than white people. The day before these figures were announced, images were emerging of a Minnesota man being suffocated to death by a police officer trying to restrain him by kneeling on his throat. His name was George Floyd. The mayor of Minnesota, visibly shaken, made a statement in which he insisted: 'being black in America should not be a death sentence'.

We have different perspectives on the world because the world behaves differently towards us. We 'act' differently with different people and in different circumstances. To each new situation we bring all kinds of attitudes and prejudices. Drama puts these power relationships into action. As in life, our characters have no choice but to carry the baggage of their identity and status. They react to the world as *it* reacts to them. There's an improvisation exercise where each actor draws a number randomly out of a hat indicating their status in the group: one is the lowest status, two higher than one, three higher than that, so on and so forth. The actors play out a scene: a party, a business meeting, a political rally … modifying their behaviour and language depending on where they're placed in the pecking order: those with higher status, for instance, tend to move less and speak softer.

Character, though, is something else. Character is not who we are in the eyes of the world, but who we are in our core. Character is defined by the choices we make *in spite* of the obstacles we face not *because* of them, *in spite* of our disadvantages or privileges, and it is this *inner character* that the audience responds to.

My grandparents were all around twenty when the Second World War began: two Jews, a half-Jew and a Catholic from Belfast. My mother's mother was a London bus conductor during the war and she loved it. She'd never have had the opportunity if the men hadn't gone off to fight. She was a Sephardi Jew from a Dutch family so she had soft olive skin that indicated her Middle Eastern heritage. This was unusual in the East End of the 1930s and 1940s so she was often taken for someone black or Asian. (It must have been strange to experience racism on behalf of a race to which you don't belong. An Armenian friend of mine often received anti-Semitic taunts in the streets that I was completely free from.) When my grandmother told people she was Jewish some people asked. 'Then where are your horns?'

In my memory she's always laughing. Even in the hospital, when she was dying of lung cancer in her fifties, she had a life force, a charisma.

Her husband, my grandfather, grew up a century ago on an East End council estate with an itinerant gambler Jewish father. An instinctive socialist, his experience during the war demolished any vestigial deference he may have had for the upper classes. 'Idiots', he would say of many his commanding officers, foisted with leadership due to a simple accident of birth. 'Couldn't organise a fuck in a brothel.'

For six years he fought in Normandy, El Alamein, and Palestine. He was a quarter master sergeant in charge of supplies, which gave him a certain cachet with the men. Gifted with numbers and an innate understanding of human psychology, he ran hundreds of little scams, apparently accruing a suitcase of cash that, despite his ingenuity, he couldn't spirit back into the UK. I think he just handed it all to the locals in Palestine before he left. He experienced hand-to-hand combat, marched 1,500 Italian prisoners of war across the desert with his mate, and was finally demobbed at the end of the war and deposited back into civilian life. 'I was good with a gun', he once told my brother and me apropos nothing when we took him for a Chinese meal. We were the same age he was when he had to use one.

After six years of fighting the Nazis, it must have been vexing to find gangs of Blackshirt fascists still menacing the streets around the East End where he'd returned home. Oswald Mosley's British Union of Fascists had been discredited after the British victory, but there were still thugs inspired by his movement taunting and attacking Jews and their houses and shops, intent on driving them out. Young people like my grandfather and my uncles, ripened by war, organised themselves into their own gangs and fought back.

My grandmother's eldest brother, whose real name was Isaac but was known to all, forever, for reasons I'm not completely sure but could take a guess at, as Jimmy the Market, was a natural bruiser and likely leader. When I heard about all this as a teenager I was squeamish about the easy violence of their resistance. I remember sitting around the Passover table arguing for the pacifist position with Jimmy's younger brother, my Uncle Lou ('youngest sergeant major in the British army!' he would bark unprompted proudly in reference to himself). 'You don't reason with fascists,' Lou instructed me. 'You hit 'em with a hard stick. That's what they understand.'

These people were bred to be tough and resilient, to be ready for a scrap at the drop of a hat. They bent the rules when they had to and were not shy about getting stuck in when the moment required. My father was the same. He had his own battles and brawls as an asthmatic kid growing up in East London in the 1950s, half Jewish half Northern Irish Catholic, half hairdresser half market-trader, half dandy half street fighter. Only a generation later and there's my brother and me immersed in books and plays and films making our living by writing and on very unfamiliar terms with the jungle laws of physical combat. Even so, in my early twenties, I intervened in a road rage incident. A few vehicles ahead of me at a slip-road junction, a man had abandoned his van mid-road to remonstrate with a station wagon that had cut him up, holding up a queue of traffic. In the station wagon was a large South Asian family, children in the back. The man, brick-solid, face purpling with indignation, took a very aggressive stance and started shouting racist abuse, even penetrating his head and torso through their car window. That was it, I thought, I'm not having that. I stuck my straw-mop head with my cheap sunglasses out of the window of my battered Honda Civic and commanded him to desist.

Immediately. And clear the road. He promptly turned on his heels and began to clomp over to me. The station wagon took its opportunity and drove off. I didn't blame them, but I wasn't concerned, I'd already modelled out the confrontation in my head. Van man and I would debate the situation and I, with my philosophy degree and right on my side, would convince him of the error of his ways, graciously accepting his grovelling apology.

Strangely that's not what happened. Before I could open my mouth a rock hard, wide-knuckled fist connected with my jaw, sending my brain and my sunglasses spinning. Character is action. When I told my father, he nodded thoughtfully and said: 'Every now and then it's good to get punched in the face.' He's always been fecund with homespun wisdom, my dad.

Anyway, back to Lew, my grandfather: Papa, we called him. He'd inherited his father's gambling instincts and had an affinity with mathematics so he became a turf accountant running books on horse races and dog races for the biggest geezers in the game, becoming intimate with some of the most notorious gangsters of the era. He played poker professionally and became something of a guru. Always dapper, always a half-smoked cigarette drifting from a lip perpetually curved into a faint, knowing smile, tall and wiry and fabulously handsome, his hair, until he died – at eighty-one – thick, jet-black and combed with military commitment. He lived in a flat off Shoot Up Hill in Kilburn where he'd once opened an early betting shop. Legend has it, unsuited to normal business hours, he sold the shop to a Polish refugee and fellow street bookie who was born Joseph Kagalitsky. Joseph Kagalitsky had changed his name to Joe Coral and that name is now emblazoned above nearly two thousand betting shops across the country. But Lew, in his heart, was a song and dance man. As a teenager he was invited to try out for the legendary music hall act Flanagan and Allen's Crazy Gang, but when his father heard about it he exploded: 'No son of mine's gonna finish up a Nancy Boy!' In those days you heeded the parent. Despite this, he carried with him always a sort of performer's panache: he walked with a dancer's gait. He was in awe of his wife and devoted to her entirely. He'd roar with laughter at the mere thought of her, then immediately explode with tears. The two were achingly glamorous, creatures of the night. Their eyes dark and fizzing, their hair shining with product, they sucked the marrow from experience as only people whose youth had been defined by war could. In his pomp Lew was a face on the London club scene, instrumental in breaking American acts like Sammy Davis Junior in the UK at venues like The Talk of The Town in Leicester Square, where he had his private table. The famous lengthy tracking shot in *Goodfellas* when Henry leads Karen through the frenetic kitchen to get to his table, deftly swung into position for him by an attentive waiter, reminds me of his description of that time.

I was about six when I saw his image appear through the frosted glass of our hallway door. His body was uncharacteristically slumped, slanted forward, the strut gone from him. He didn't say a word, just stood there: a carrier bag hung at the end of each lifeless arm, and I knew immediately that my grandmother was dead. Too young to understand, I regarded this scene with detached curiosity, like I was watching a mime-show, but somehow, somewhere inside, I knew our world had definitively changed. My mother was sobbing uncontrollably, helpless with tears. Later I realised why: at thirty, with two small boys, a father broken by grief, and a husband preoccupied by a volatile and struggling family business, she was the one who was in charge now.

Character is action and action is its own language. My grandfather's hunched stillness communicated his meaning with absolute clarity. The bad version of this scene, the hacky version, would have the same actions overlaid with dialogue telling the same story. As sort of doubling up of the emotion.

The slightly better version would let the action reveal the subtext and the words push against it: words of optimism in the darkness, consoling, but mendacious talk of an easeful passing. The good version would reveal a quality the characters didn't even know they possessed: a quality that shone through regardless of their troubles.

Soon after his wife died, my grandfather started to lose his sight. His eyes were ravaged by a perfect storm of glaucoma and macula degeneration. The first time he used his NHS-issued white stick he was crossing a road precariously and an impatient driver shouted 'blind bastard!' He never used the stick again. He didn't want to appear vulnerable. He didn't want to be defined by this disability and resolved to carry on with his life as if he didn't have one.

'Call 'em out!' he used to shout, which, depending on the situation, meant reading him the TV listings or the menu, or whatever. He was famous among poker players at his regular haunt, the Victoria Casino for singing during the game in an attempt to cover a bad hand, and he carried on this tradition even as his blindness took hold, peering at the cards through the net-curtain fuzziness of his fading sight, holding them right up to his face. They called him Lew 'Singalong' Saltsman until the day he died.

In her TED talk the Nigerian-born novelist Chimamanda Ngozi Adichie warns of the danger of the single story. Power, she argues, is the ability not just to tell the story of another person, but to make *that* the *definitive version* of that person. 'The problem with stereotypes', she says, 'is not that they are untrue, but that they are incomplete. They rob people of dignity. It makes the recognition of our equal humanity difficult. It emphasizes how we are different, rather than how we are similar.' We become merciful, says the American philosopher Martha Nussbaum, when we understand each human being's life as 'a complex narrative in a world full of obstacles'.

EXERCISE 3: Think of a person whose voice you know well. This person should be, or have been, very present in your life. It could be a mother or father, or sibling or friend, lover or work colleague, anyone whose voice you'd be able, without very much effort, to summon to your mind. Then write a monologue in the voice of this person. In this monologue this person should be talking directly to you about an issue they feel particular exercised or vehement about. Again there's no need for a shape, or a resolution, it can begin and end at any point. The exercise has to be executed with an element of spontaneity: don't spend too much time contemplating your choices, go with your initial instincts.

Combining the specific idiosyncrasies of human expression and desire, with your own innate sense of shape and rhythm, incites you to write a piece that necessarily contains complex dimensions. Or to use Matt Ridley's analogy, the creative impulse has sex with a stored experience and a living entity is brought into being.

My play *Filthy Business* began with Yetta Solomon and her grandson Mickey yoked together in the family-owned shop before opening. Money has been stolen from the cash machine and Yetta, suspecting Mickey knows the guilty party, is trying to wheedle information out of him.

> **Yetta**   Bastard son bitch. How could dey do dis? Seventy
> quids taken from da till. Now. When we're in *schtuck*! When
> we're fighting to keep da dogs from da door, *now* dey take
> from us? Well we gotta fight back boychick. We gotta
> protect ourselves or we look like chumps, you understand?
> Sure you understand, you know what's what. (*Closing in on
> him conspiratorially.*) So. You gonna tell who's da teef?

> **Mickey**   Me?

Nothing has come easily to Yetta, and here, in this early moment, we witness her facility for manipulating emotion, for planting the seeds of terror into her victims and cornering them until they have no choice but to give her what she wants.

What she *wants* is to preserve the family business. We discover that she was driven out of her home as a youngster and lost her whole family to genocide. She arrived in Britain and built a new life. The shop has become her haven and allowed her to be autonomous, to be the ruler of her own universe: to her, saving her family from danger means saving the business from going under. To add to her sense of alienation, she has a rather elastic relationship with the English language. A refugee determined to assert her status as a British citizen, Yetta's speech has a particular cadence and power. Every time she speaks she reveals her origins and so her desires.

When the mighty Sara Kestelman played her in Edward Hall's fabulously gritty production at Hampstead Theatre, the audience understood immediately what was at stake.

But while Yetta wants to save the business for her grandchild, Mickey, he conversely wants to break out. He wants to reject the destiny written for him before birth of being a 'Rubber Man'. 'I want to be a ladies hairdresser', he finally confesses, sending Yetta into a paroxysm of confusion and rage. This contest of wills is then played out over the next two hours and across two decades. The conflicting desires of these two determined characters impacts on everyone around them and makes up the architecture of the play. The drama of the play is composed of characters with definitive but opposing *wants*: characters in *conflict*.

4 Conflict

In Neil Simon's *Broadway Bound*, elder brother Stan keeps asking younger brother Eugene what he thinks is the essential ingredient in comedy. '*Conflict!*' he shouts. Then he asks what the other key ingredient is, Eugene panics and answers '*More conflict?*'

The impresario Stephen Joseph apparently believed that a comedy is where someone eventually gets what they want, and a tragedy is where they don't. In between there's the same dynamic. 'In every comedy', continues Stan, 'even drama, somebody has to want something and want it bad. When somebody tries to stop him – that's conflict.'

Tennessee Williams begins his play *Cat on A Hot Tin Roof* with the icy exchanges of married couple Brick and Maggie, as they get ready for a party. Maggie is trying to warn her husband that his brother and sister-in-law have been conspiring against him, buttering up wealthy, dying Big Daddy in order to elbow Brick out of his rightful inheritance. She thinks their lack of children is counting against them in the eyes of the dying patriarch, so she tries to elicit sexual intimacy from him so that they can create an heir.

Brick remains stubbornly remote. He says and does very little, but that doesn't mean he doesn't express vast oceans of feeling: bitterness, regret, revulsion, incarceration – his silence begins to scream at us.

Williams creates a simmering tension because both of these characters desperately want directly contradictory things. Maggie aches for affection, and yearns for a child. Brick wants nothing more (or less!) than to be left alone. He wants oblivion: he wants to numb himself to his acute feelings of self-loathing by drinking until he hears the click in his head and his senses shut down. Maggie wants him to care, to *feel*. Brick desperately wants *not* to feel.

While Maggie is full of life and charisma, desperately active, desperately yearning, Brick's 'lack of wanting' seems to lend his character a magnetism that gathers momentum through the play. It's sort of *active negative*. Life has disappointed and deceived him and he's fallen into a paralysis of despair. Like Hamlet, the more he rejects the world and withdraws into himself, the more compelling he becomes.

Williams knows his characters don't have to be directly at odds or fighting or raging at each other to create dramatic conflict. He writes about people teetering on the edge of collapse, people using all their strength and guile to keep from falling into the abyss. There is, though, with his characters, and this is crucial, always the tiniest hope that they can change. That even as the odds are stacked against them the hope exists, vain as that hope might be, that they can somehow control and alter their circumstances. If only they could get this one person to do the one thing they appear determined not to do. That's how you wring comedy and tragedy out of a single situation.

Characters in a situation of conflict are like chicks about to hatch. The egg is cracking. The slender membrane holding it together is about to be ripped apart. The ground trembles and quakes. The drama is made up of the moments before the detonation.

In David Eldridge's exquisite two-hander *Beginning*, Laura and Danny want the same thing. Each other. Various past indignities, modern-life anxieties and general self consciousness, however, serve to block their shared desire and they spend the entire evening in a sort of awkward dance, moving variously closer together and further apart, until, finally, making the much anticipated physical connection. Once they make this physical connection, the detonation happens, the egg is hatched, and the play is over.

EXERCISE 4: The Job Interview. An improvisation. Two chairs, two characters: interviewer, already seated, and interviewee. The interviewer is under pressure to appoint someone and wrap up the interview quickly: perhaps they have somewhere they urgently need to be. The interviewee, immediately prior to their interview, receives some devastating, possibly life-changing news that will completely flummox and disorient them, but also means getting this job is even more important.

When you come to write a scene, the more specific the characters' predicament, the more concentrated their desire, the more alive the scene will be. Neil Simon said: 'by the time you know your conflicts, the play is already written in your mind. All you have to do is put the words down.' But where is all this conflict leading? What crash are these characters heading for that will transform their fortunes and change them forever?

5 Reversal

for tis the sport to have the enginer
Hoist with his owne petar.
Hamlet

EXERCISE 5: Another version of the job interview scenario is that the interviewee (who desperately needs the job) and the interviewer (who is under pressure to fill the position) discover when they meet that they knew each other in the past. In that past, the interviewee had power over the interviewer, but now that power has shifted. How does this play out?

In 2009 I was in my thirties. Screen and radio writing was sustaining me and I was becoming, what's known in the business as, established. But I was reaching a crossroads in my life. I'd had plays on at the Menier Chocolate Factory and Hampstead Theatre, but was being drawn more and more away from the theatre and into the world of television series and development. This was in a time just before the explosion of ambition and innovation of the current golden age of TV, but the seeds were being planted. I'd had a film on Channel 4 about Saddam Hussein's last days in power and had written on the final season of *Robin Hood* for BBC One, but I felt I needed to get back to my first love. However, I didn't have an idea for a play and couldn't see where to go next.

It was February. London was drizzly, downbeat and dark, it matched my mood. I went to see Richard Bean's play *England People Very Nice* and, at the interval, Sebastian Born, the National Theatre's literary associate, approached me and said: 'Will you have a cup of tea with me tomorrow?' Sometimes, in the theatre, a cup of tea is just a cup of tea. Sometimes it's a profound moment of change in a writer's life. This cup of tea was of the latter variety. We met in the foyer outside the coffee shop, the same spot I would meet Philip Arditti only a couple of years later, and, after patiently listening to me droning on about my work anxieties, he said, 'I actually asked you here for a reason.'

It had landed in my inbox by the time I got home later that day. It was a large, almost impenetrably complex document: Catherine Grosvenor's meticulous literal translation of a Polish play called *Our Class*. I printed out a hard copy and took it down to my local café, The Fat Deli, at that time a mash-up of tapas bar and brunch spot run by a gruff Yorkshireman called Lee with high standards and a low tolerance for crying children and nit-picking philistines. I ordered myself a cappuccino (as it comes, no frills) and sat down to read. The playwright Tadeusz Slobodzianek had based his play on Jan Gross's book *Neighbours*. It was an account of the massacre of the Jewish half of the small village of Jedwabne by the Catholic half during the Second World War and the continuing collective denial of Polish involvement. The play had not been staged in his native country or, in fact, anywhere. Nick Hytner had come to it via the director of the Habima Theatre, who said: you're the only ones who can do this. The first production, in my version at the Cottesloe, came in 2009, nine years after Tadeusz had first read *Neighbours*.

Ten years on, there have been productions of the play all over the world and multiple academic papers.

'We're going to do it in the Cottesloe in September. Bijan Sheibani's on board to direct. Fancy doing a version?' Sebastian Born is not a man who minces his words. He was handing me my first show at the National Theatre in the most casual way possible. Still, I was reticent. I'd written about terrorism and Jewish identity in *Weinstein*, about a Holocaust denier in *The Glass Room*, about slaughter and betrayal in Saddam Hussein's Iraq, and I was apprehensive about diving back into the controversial arena of racial conflict, war and genocide. I sipped my Fat Deli cappuccino (perfection, God I loved that place) and started reading.

Catherine's translation was itself a huge accomplishment. While staying faithful to the literal meaning of each line, she was often able to give alternative options. So if a phrase seemed indecipherable even once translated, which it often did, she would suggest within her text various additional words and phrases that could be closely related, but clearer to an English speaker. So even though the play felt very alien to me at first, a close study allowed the material to emerge.

Our Class is about ghosts. It's about how traumas of the past can never be buried. It's about the corrosive nature of denial and the exorcising of demons and it's about the way political and religious ideology can violently divide people. Slobodzianek had been inspired by the work of another polish theatre maker Tadeusz Kantor, whose *Dead Class* is about attempting to revisit childhood to make sense of past traumas. In *Our Class* we follow ten classmates from innocent children dreaming of their future, to clammily ideological teenagers to young adults simultaneously in love and at war. The play could have ended at the climactic burning of the Jewish members of the class in a barn, but it doesn't. Like life, it continues. The characters that survive are forced to live with the horror, live with the ghosts. This, for me, was the whole point.

The action of *Our Class* is played out in a sort of liminal space, a neutral mid-ground where characters can freely give testimony one moment and then hurl themselves into the action the next. It's an act of expiation: at once a purging and a remembering. The characters unburden themselves before us. They've witnessed far more of life than they'd bargained for and now they need absolution. And the confessional nature of the play draws the audience into complicity with them. Further, the multi-protagonist narrative becomes the dramatic delivery system for the competing versions of the same harrowing stories. In this way it challenges conventional notions of victim and perpetrator.

In spite of all this, it was quite late in that first reading at the Fat Deli that the play suddenly leapt out and grabbed me by the throat. In the third quarter of the story the womanising opportunist Menachem, who'd escaped the slaughter of his fellow Jews, is compelled to return home to hunt down the perpetrators and become their torturer. These were his classmates. They raped his wife and burned her and his child alive. Now, instead of cowering in fear and running, he finds himself interrogating these frightened, weasel-like people even as they plead with him for mercy. All Menachem feels is a filthy, pitiless loathing. When I came to this moment in the play I was almost breathless. Victim had become persecutor. A sharp reversal of fortunes has occurred. The reward for Menachem's survival was to become almost as vicious and merciless as his tormentors and the perverse complexity of the human condition was here, for me, made manifest. These are the moments we must seek to find in the stories we write for the stage.

Though much of our work is done with a sort of semi-conscious fervour, there does come a crucial moment when you have to impose your creative and technical will on the characters. It's the pivotal moment in the play when you have to force them to confront the consequences of their actions. Take Oedipus.

Newly enthroned as King of Thebes and full of *hubris*, he promises the people he will destroy the cause of the plague that bedevils the kingdom. He is, of course, blind to the fact that he himself is the cause (even when he is warned by the actually blind Tiresias). When he finally sees clearly and discovers he'd accidentally killed his father and married his mother the knowledge is too much to bear and he puts out his eyes. The sudden seismic shift from positive to negative is the key dramatic event of the play. The audience is forced to empathise with the character as his fortunes plummet, but the catharsis comes because Oedipus himself has willed his fate into being. By pursuing his desired objective with a compulsive determination, he has brought about this personal catastrophe.

Andre Gide said 'the structure of your play is always the story of the birds coming home to roost'. In *All My Sons*, the dark truth about the crime Joe Keller committed as he tried to keep his business afloat during the Second World War is only revealed when George, the son of his business partner (who took the fall for the faulty plane engines), arrives like an avenging angel. When George finally reveals the truth, all the characters in the play are forced to confront their own complicity in the denial.

In *Filthy Business* the central character Yetta begins the play with the words '*I believe in to punish.*' Because Yetta has spent her life on the offensive, when the business eventually fails and the vultures circle the younger generations want to break free. Unwilling to release her grip, she engineers an arson attack on the shop in order to collect on the insurance and frighten her family into falling in line. The fire ruins the health of her sons, shatters their already precarious trust in each other and, finally, brings about the end of the business and the family name. Her actions lead to the opposite outcome to the initial desire that drove her. The punishment she believes in is meted out to her.

Reversals don't always have to be so directly self-inflicted. An expectation can be constructed in an audience's mind like a mental picture, only to be shifted a few degrees to reveal a whole new reality, and thus upend entirely our perspective on the same event. About five years ago I had dropped my daughter off at school when I received a panicked, breathless phone call from my mother. 'Ryan!' she cried. 'They're beheading people in Edgware!' My mother's always had a flair for catching the listener's attention.

At the time, reports of Islamic terrorists beheading hostages in the Middle East had become regular and disturbing headlines. For my mother, who always lived on the precipice of catastrophe, it was only a matter of time before the practice became commonplace in North London. She and my father had driven to their local cemetery to visit some family graves, but were prevented from entering by a police cordon. Trying a separate entrance, they met a farmer who told them he'd seen, 'with his own eyes', lying in the road, a man's decapitated head.

My first instinct was to turn to Google. If such a terrifying and tremorous event had occurred, surely somebody somewhere would be discussing it? I found nothing. 'Are you sure this was an act of terrorism Mum?' I asked. 'What else could it be?' she insisted. I could hear my exasperated father in the background confessing that they knew nothing, had seen nothing and they were now going home. I got on with my day and forgot about it.

Later, I checked Google once more and found that a man had committed suicide in Edgware, near the Jewish cemetery. He tied a rope around his neck, tied the rope to a tree and drove at speed. His head was severed in the process. The incident had no connection whatsoever to the cemetery or to international terrorism. It was a man's desperate final act.

There's an equation when revealing a piece of information in a drama. It's not a, but b. It's not what you thought (a), but something you hadn't anticipated, but is equally plausible (b). There's a distance between what was expected and what transpires. And the greater that distance, the greater the power the reversal has.

One of the most thrilling reversals in contemporary drama can be found in Lucy Kirkwood's *Chimerica*. The play begins in a hotel room overlooking Tiananmen Square on 5 June 1989. Joe Schofield, an American photojournalist, witnesses a young Chinese protestor, a small bag in his hand, standing before a military tank. Acting on instinct, Joe grabs his camera, takes a few snaps, and seals his place in photographic history.

The main action of the play, though, takes place more than twenty years later. The 'Tank Man' snap has become iconic and made Joe internationally famous, but when he discovers a coded message in a newspaper, he develops a dreadful feeling that the photograph that made his career might also have destroyed its subject. Obsessed with discovering the truth he ends up at The Glorious City Flower Shop. The owner, Pengsi, is cagey and obstructive, but Joe presses the Tank Man photograph under his nose and says: 'Is he your brother?' An argument ensues that escalates into a vicious fight. Joe gets slapped, shoved, Pengsi spits in his face, but Joe's in this to the death, he'll suffer any pain or ignominy to get to the truth. Joe demands to know if 'Tank Man' is alive. Finally, admitting the truth, Pengsi shakes his head, no. Joe doesn't want to believe the man is really dead. The guilt is too much. He pushes the photo toward Pengsi again, hoping against hope for a different outcome. 'Are you sure?' Joe pleads pointing to the student holding the bag standing in front of the tank. 'Look. This man, you're sure he's not –'

And then comes the *coup de grace*. It's a heart-stopping moment both for the audience and the character. Pengsi looks at the figure Joe is indicating and says: 'I don't know about this man.' And, moving Joe's finger from the protestor to the soldier, the man whose head is seen peeking out over the top of the tank, says: '*This* man. Here. The soldier. In the tank, *he* was my brother. Unknown hero, my brother' (my italics).

Pengsi goes on to explain that his brother was executed because he refused to fire on an unarmed civilian. That's why he's a hero. In that moment Joe's, and our, conception of heroism is deepened forever. It's electric because the audience experiences an instant and profound shift of perspective at precisely the same instant as the character. We suddenly realise we have been looking at the world through the wrong lens. The play forces us to step back, to zoom out. It shifts the world on its axis and makes us see it differently. Makes us *feel* it differently.

Remember how, when you were a child, you had the most intense fascination for the smallest things? How losing a toy or being told off could feel like the most cataclysmic event? Remember how, when you were a teenager, the fragmenting of a cherished friendship could feel like the ground shattering under your feet? Remember how the world was so contained when you were younger? When you're very young your world is smaller. You can see the borders of your finite territory with a naked eye and you feel safe inside them. But that means when things go wrong within those borders it has a cosmic significance. Great drama needn't have geopolitical dimensions: if the consequences are profound for the character they will be for us too.

In Shakespeare's *The Winter's Tale*, Leontes, in an erroneous fit of jealous rage, condemns his wife Hermione and, by association, her baby daughter to death. When the child, saved from the waves, returns home as an adult decades later, the truth of Hermione's innocence emerges and the world shifts, this time from negative to positive. Hermione's frozen body comes back to life: '*she's warm!*' Leontes realises the error of his ways and reconciliation is now possible.

Reconciliation, then, becomes the product of the action of the play. Tension leads to conflict, conflict to a combustible reversal, and that reversal peels away a new reality, a *truer* reality through a character's realisation of a deeper truth. Through these reversals a play can move us to a wider understanding of the human condition, to a better appreciation of our own potential as a species.

6 Reaction

A play unravels in front of the audience in real time. That means stage time has a special quality. I think it's why we go to the theatre: to experience the suspension of the normal rules of the physical world. Within that suspended state there are infinite possibilities.

Aristotle says there is no such thing as 'the now'. Or rather that now is not a part of time, but a boundary between the past and the future. The theatre exists on this boundary line, in this sliver of 'non-time'. It gives the experience a special kind of intensity. It can also, for that reason, have a special kind of irritation. Time can slow to a grinding, interminable pace in the theatre and a bad play can be spectacularly tedious. But when a play works, when it *connects*, it can transport you.

What's more, the theatre's live-ness and immediacy means that the same actors performing the same play in the same production in the same space can be a totally different experience for different people and on different nights. I've seen this divergence with my own eyes many times: A show that elicits hoots of laughter and cheers at the curtain one night can play to bemused silence and polite tinkling applause the next. Once an audience gathers to watch a show a chemical reaction occurs between it and the actors.

During the pandemic, online filmed versions of hit plays have sustained audiences aching for the unique vitality of a theatre production. It reminds us how wildly popular good work for the stage can be. But these are really ghostly echoes of a glorious past. Theatre's fleeting impermanence is part of what makes it special and the existence of a live audience is what makes it theatre. Unless we feel the heat of another body next to us, unless we see the sweat and spit of the actors and they feel the quality of our concentration, it isn't theatre.

In quantum physics there's a concept called The Observer Effect. It's the theory that a phenomenon is fundamentally altered the moment it's observed. When you check your car's tyre pressure you have to let out some of the air first to take the measurement: So the tyre's pressure is changed because it was measured. Similarly, we can only see an object when light hits it causing it to reflect that light.

Imagine you were being intensely watched while performing a simple task. Say a group of people gather in your kitchen and focus their full attention on you as you make a cup of tea. Maybe your body stiffens, maybe your gestures become bigger, more deliberate. You act differently because you're being watched.

I never understood productions that desperately urged their audience to call out or come up on stage to participate. We're already participating: we're *there*. We're fundamentally, physiologically altering the performance itself. And because multiple timescales can exist simultaneously on stage; because multiple locations and states of being can constantly criss-cross, often existing at the same instance – a feat only possible in the theatre because of its live-ness; because of its presence in front of you in that moment, this special quality can not be replicated in any other art form.

This live-ness, of course, also means that, while, as a playwright, you exert a god-like power over your characters while you're writing, the moment the play gets in front of an audience you're chillingly helpless. I've seen actors in my plays forget lines and make up entire speeches. I've seen an actor spill a full cup of water over the stage and, pupils widening in panic, aware his fellow actors had to dance across that area in the next scene, stop the show by crying out '*mop!*' I've seen an actor, after missing their cue, leap on stage half-dressed to begin the scene midway through (presumably applying the lunatic logic that the narrative had continued without him and must now be a few pages down the road). One particularly gutsy young actor in a New Zealand production of *Filthy Business* spent a whole performance sick with food poisoning and sprinting off stage mid-scene to throw up in a bucket, before running back on to perform with perky brilliance only to then run off again the other side. They had buckets on both wings.

One night, as a play of mine (*What We Did To Weinstein*) was about to start, a megawatt TV and theatre star, there to see the show with his entire family, became embroiled in a full-blown fistfight over his seats with a member of the public. This had the effect of holding up the start of the show. A latecomer being ushered in, assuming this was part of the play, said: 'Oh, I didn't know *he* was in it. I *like* him.' During that same production, the late, great Harry Towb (playing a famous dying writer and, in his eighties, giving a master-class in how to be a human being and artist), at a particularly poignant moment, extravagantly broke wind. The guff ripped flagrantly across the stage and reduced his fellow performers to fits of giggles. They juddered on in that vein to the end of the performance. In the dressing room after, Harry said to them with a wry twinkle, 'did you hear that? I did a massive fart.' 'No, no', they assured him, 'we didn't hear a thing.'

Other stories are legion. During rehearsals for a recent production of *Uncle Vanya*, a famously flamboyant actor playing Vanya gesticulated a little too enthusiastically and accidently poked his Doctor Astrov in the eye. Astrov, being played by an actor known for his brooding masculinity, screamed like a baby seal and bolted from the theatre clutching his face. Astrov's wounds were tended to and, soldier that he was, he was back on stage the next night with accompanying eye patch.

Unfortunately, however, as he was delivering one of his recondite Chekhovian speeches, unbalanced by his restricted sight, he misjudged the edge of the stage, lost his footing and tumbled headfirst into the front row. Console yourself with the knowledge that even Mr Chekhov could not have foreseen this turn of events while writing his play.

In the theatre the actors are on the front line. Every night your play is on, they are out there representing your work. Love them. The theatre begins and ends with them. Give them great stuff to do. Give them things to do and things to say that are better than anything they can make up on their own. Once you've done that, take a breath, unclench your grip and get out of their way. Trust them with your darlings. Let the actors be, as Peter Brook wrote, the instruments of the play, not the tools, and they will bring it to vivid life.

Writing for the stage can be a fraught business. If you're lucky you fail only 90 per cent of the time. But on those precious few occasions when you sit in the audience for one of your plays and listen to laughter, or hear a collective gasp, or sense a group of strangers bend toward the stage as one, swept up in a sort of synchronised intensity, emotionally conjoined in space and time, it's absolutely thrilling. Being in a theatre audience is an act of solidarity. One is more actively complicit in the experience of the drama in theatre than in any other medium, and that's what makes that initial moment when the lights go down so infused with anticipation.

The critic, of course, judges a play by a totally different set of criteria. They want to know what new thing the play is saying, how it's reinventing the form, or what burning issue is being addressed. They've got to post their 500-word copy and can't afford to give in to the collective euphoria. Their solemn task is to cast a cold, disinterested eye on the work and report their findings to their readers. That's the theory anyway. Many critics do indeed get carried away by the collective euphoria, become seduced by the latest hot thing. Rarely, though, are they altered by the experience. A play is a living, changing thing and as an audience member you feel instantly complicit. The intimate, immediate, shared and reciprocal nature of a live performance of a text can make the quality of that experience so intense we feel changed by it.

Good critics are rare. They try to push the artists to stretch themselves, to fulfill their potential. They're candid about the work in spite of the prevailing fashions: they go to the theatre with hope. Even if they play is not really meant for them, few people sit in an auditorium and think: 'I really hope the next two hours of my life is a horrible waste of time.' But, like the rest of us, critics like to have their aesthetic and political preconceptions flattered. When my first play *Happy Savages* was playing at the Hammersmith Lyric Studio, a group of small round white men in small round black glasses descended on the theatre with their small leather notebooks. At the interval I saw them all huddled together in a scrum scratching their chins and discussing the first half. They all, I noticed, wore pallid and clammy jacket and trouser combos that matched their pallid and clammy skin. It was August. This was their summer-wear. During the second half, while the audience immersed themselves in the play, the small round men scribbled. Their broadsheet minds already made up, they were plucking lines from the play to serve the view they'd settled on and thus sealed the production's fate.

The world's changed significantly, print media has given way to online reviews and bloggers from a much more diverse range of writers, but the problem remains the same. Theatre is meant to be a shared experience: criticism demands you separate yourself from the group. What's more the critic comes to the theatre in myriad states of mind: after a difficult conversation or a small triumph or a lovers' tiff or on the cusp of a new opportunity or in the embers of a terrible fall-out or in a foul temper or after a spectacular meal, and they carry that mood with them into the auditorium. Because their trade means they must be the observer rather than the participant, they rarely allow themselves to be swept along by the action. Perhaps this goes some way to explaining why there's often a bifurcation between critical reactions and audience responses. It's because they're having two separate experiences of the same play.

But while it's always been an occupational hazard for theatre makers that they live their professional lives cheek by jowl with the people who assess their work and send that assessment out into the world, the playwright must shut out those thoughts. However desirable it is to be adulated in the national press, we must resist writing to please the critics. *It is the play that must have a relationship with the audience, not the practitioner with the critic.*

EXERCISE 6: Write two fantasy reviews of the play you envisage creating. The first should be bad. A damning, excoriating one-star massacre: the worst conceivable critique of your work. Be brutal. Be as unpleasant as possible. Slate yourself. Imagine the most loathsome, irritable version of yourself watching this atrocious pile-up and let rip. Then write the good one. The kind of breathless, cloying rave you'd donate a healthy organ to receive. This exercise can be a very cathartic and informative experience. It can reveal surprising things about how you see yourself and your writing, about what you're trying to achieve, as well as pinpointing some of the pitfalls you might run into with your play and isolating some of the limitations you might have as a writer.

If you're a playwright starting out in the theatre today, your manuscript will pass through many hands before it reaches the eyes and ears of an audience and reviewers: agents, dramaturges, literary managers, producers and directors, casting agents and actors, marketing and publicity departments. Many of these people will see it as their job to pass comment on your work, to advise on where to go with it and suggest amendments. Be open, but be cautious. A dramaturge, for instance, can have their uses. They've taken countless plays apart and put them back together and they are in constant touch with theatre managements regarding issues of changing tastes and subject matter. But because the play starts somewhere deep in your unconscious and evolves in your mind over time, sometimes over decades, while an outside eye can be helpful, it can never replace you as the ultimate creator of your work. It's also worth bearing in mind that what theatres are so often looking for is a unique voice: a play that comes from a totally original place with a powerful individual vision.

The screenwriting titan William Goldman's advice regarding notes is the best I can offer. He talks of a story having a spine. If the spine is strong and constant, the script can absorb any additions and subtractions *ad infinitum* without collapsing. If the spine is chipped away at or removed altogether the story won't succeed. It's the writer's job to protect the spine of their story. In my view, the spine of a play is its clarity of intention, attend to that and your play will connect.

The first preview of *Games For Lovers* at the Vaults has arrived. You dive down a narrow, cobbled slip road and descend into the mouth of a cavernous cellar underneath the concourse at Waterloo Station. (Coincidentally where, sixty years previously, my father would pack up the family rubber stall when, as a boy, he worked on the market in Lower Marsh.) This play was written almost by accident. It grew unexpectedly. You never know which of your embryonic ideas is going develop arms and legs, and organs and features and make its way in the world, but now, here we are, the set built, the lights focused, the music written, the audience taking their seats and the actors waiting in the wings.

The first night of any new play is always electric. The theatre's a Large Hadron Collider: two elemental forces, production and audience, are about to be smashed together in the same space and time. The results are unpredictable, but the newness of it always thrills. The first performance of *Our Class* will stay with me forever. In the final moments of the first half a young Jewish woman, Dora, addresses the audience. In the previous hour or so we have seen her humiliated, raped by her schoolmates, beaten by her neighbours, abandoned by her husband, and corralled into a barn with her infant child, to be locked up and burnt to death. She turns to us and says this.

> **Dora** It got dark from the smoke. People started crying and screaming. Then choking. Why were they doing this? Zygmunt said we were to going to the Ghetto tomorrow. Liar! Someone was clawing at my head and pulling my hair. I dropped the baby. Someone hit me. Why Rysiek? I realized I was treading on someone. And someone was treading on me. And Menachem, he was probably off with one of his sluts. I started coughing and spluttering … gagging on the smoke. Then I wet myself. This is life?

In that very first preview, the first time *Our Class* had ever been performed in front of an audience in any country and in any language, we had no idea what impact it would have. Working with various actors in a number of workshops at the NT Studio, Bijan, with the help of musicians, designer Bunny Christie, and others, had whittled away any fuss or adornment to find a style that was bald, direct and simple and would give primacy to the story. The text grew hand in hand with the production and had seemed utterly appropriate at the time, but it was still a risk. You never know what will happen when audience and production collide. Sinead Matthews, playing Dora, delivered her speech with such a delicate, nuanced and almost matter-of-fact touch, it was subtly devastating. When she finished and the house lights came up for half-time, the audience seemed to have no response at all. It sat frozen in silence, holding its breath for what seemed like an eternity. I don't remember a silence quite like it in the theatre. It was a sort of clock-stopping stasis.

I remember turning to my wife and whispering: 'they hate it'. She shook her head. 'I don't think they do.' The audience were fixed to their seats in funereal respect. Eventually, there was a mechanical smattering of applause, a collective exhaling, and finally they rose and drifted into the bar, where they continued not to speak. The British interval tradition of a quick hand and a dash for the bar was abandoned for an uneasy and reflective nothingness. That nothingness was as powerful a response to a play as any I'd personally experienced.

I remember locking eyes with Bijan in that interval bar with relief: both of us knowing the risk had paid off and that we had served Tadeusz's extraordinary vision. It took me back to our very first meeting about the play. *Our Class* is a gift for a director who wants to stamp their personality onto a production. The text has very little stage direction and demands constant theatrical invention. Bijan wasn't thirty yet and this was his National Theatre debut. 'How do you plan to do it', I asked him. He shrugged. 'No idea'. 'Great', I said. Bijan's instinct not to apply a formula to such complex material was sensible. He wanted to begin the exploration with a completely open mind. Like Pinter he wanted to follow his nose and see where the play was leading.

How do we find the kind of confidence we need to trust our own instincts in this way? In the next chapter I want to look at the need to explore our personal background and qualities in order to unearth our unique dramatic voice. Without that voice, our play will never find its way to the stage. Will never live.

3 Voice

You step off the carriage and walk out of the train station, and quickly you find yourself in a world that's slightly *other*. On the surface the place appears to have been preserved in aspic for several centuries. It's about a fifteen-minute walk from Windsor and Eton Riverside station to the college and you walk past the centuries-old buildings and bijou *olde*-world style shops and cafés and pubs, and very soon you start spotting them in the distance. They appear in ones and twos at first, then flocking together in groups. Squint and they look like long, slim emperor penguins, their high collars and long tails, their eyes glistening with healthy self-regard: what journalist and ex-Etonian James Wood called, in his *London Review of Books* article, the 'air of "effortless superiority"'.

'Don't believe everything you've heard about Eton', the English master had said to me over the phone as he instructed me to present myself, on arrival, at the Porter's Lodge. This seemed to me, at first at least, like a strangely defensive appeal from a senior master at such a celebrated and established institution. I was, however, about to find out what he meant.

Our sense of ourselves, our place in the world, our sensitivity to how others perceive us is fundamental to our identity, and will, in one way or another, be reflected in our creative output. However, though it's inescapable, there is, for me, a question of how much we allow the facts of our background and upbringing, our privilege or disadvantage, to define us.

Every year the National Theatre's Learning Department organises an extraordinary event called New Views. Practising playwrights travel to schools around the country to work with and support students interested in the process of writing plays. Over the years that I've contributed to this scheme, I'm happy to report that the number of young people showing an interest in our craft is large and growing. This is particularly encouraging as it isn't included in the curriculum, so those taking part are genuinely curious and doing it in their precious spare time. That, of course, makes them much easier to help.

On this occasion I had been allocated Eton and so here I was. All the schools I'd visited up until that time had been state funded so I was surprised, when I got my small list of about four or five schools for that year, to find the words Eton College on it. I remember checking with someone in the Learning Department at the National Theatre that this was in fact the same Eton College I was thinking of. 'Yup', they said. 'That Eton.' I arrived at the Porters Lodge, a neat cubbyhole nestled within a medieval-looking archway. A garrulous, ruddy-faced figure in belt and braces behind a long desk seemed to be expecting me. He was both faintly amused and mildly suspicious by my credentials. '*National Theatre* eh?' 'Uhm, that's right.' 'You need a pass', he said, handing it to me and jabbing his finger at a sofa: 'Wait there. The master will be here presently.'

There's something potent about these insider protocols. The formalities, the outfits, ritualising: all this connects the current moment to the distant past and gives us a sense of continuity. Humans crave that. We crave the solid ground it gives us, it helps us make sense of where we are and where we're going. At Eton these codes are deeply woven into the fabric of everyday life. One rumour persists that pupils are expected to circumnavigate the school courtyard with the statue of the college founder Henry VI to their left 'so that the king is kept closest to their hearts'. It's a deeply theatrical one, but apparently, according to one former pupil, physically implausible.

Of course the theatre itself is littered with its own rites and superstitions. There's the first day meet-and-greet, the model box presentation, the technical jargon, the transformational costume fitting (I can't count the number of times I've witnessed an actor find a single item of clothing, a pair of shoes or even a wig, and suddenly realised they'd finally 'found' the character), the first night thank-you cards, the press-night party, not to mention all the personal anxieties and ghosts that bedevil us. Along with these rituals come hierarchies. The theatre is a collaborative process but that doesn't mean it's a democratic one. There is also still, in the British theatre, I'm happy to report, residual deference toward the words of the playwright. The words rule. And it's the playwright's job to be their gatekeeper. During rehearsals of *Our Class*, for instance, the staff director Ellen McDougall contacted me to say that one of the actors, Edward Hogg (playing Jakub Katz), had asked if, on his line

> What would you know about it you half-wit? You think
> you're fit for America? You'll be lucky to end up on a kibbutz.
> In the desert. Planting cactuses!

he could say 'cacti' instead of 'cactuses'. I said I had to think about it. I wasn't being insufferably grand; there are actually good reasons for the pedantry. How does the changing number of syllables affect the rhythm of the line? How does his use of Latin change the attitude of the character to the moment and the attitude of the audience toward the character? The line *was* changed in the end – the actor, I have discovered, almost always knows better than I do – but the respect for the writer's turf, the *words*, is key here. We must defend that territory jealously. Our job doesn't finish when we hand over the play. We need to keep a close eye on the detail until the very last.

It's not just in Britain that we find particular traditions. A few years ago I spent a month in Germany observing at the Schauspiel Frankfurt in a playwright exchange for the National. I saw more than thirty plays of wildly varying quality, from the movingly original (like the amazing *Winterreise* by Elfriede Jelinek) to the fantastically dull and gruesomely appetite-supressing. The attitude toward the playwright there is vastly different. The text that is delivered by the writer is seen as a starting point rather than the artefact itself. It is seen as a seed from which the interpretive artists, director, dramaturge, designer, actors, musicians construct and create the work of art. Everything is up for grabs; there isn't the sort of sacred protecting and serving of the author's vision we have in Britain and so the unique voice of the writer is often lost in the melee.

That said, some of our most prominent writers have been embraced by German theatre: Sarah Kane, Dennis Kelly and Simon Stephens, all of whom have very distinctive voices rooted potently in their own specific experience, but leave a certain complex ambiguity of structural intention in their plays that appeals to this system of making theatre. Indeed, this interpretive tradition, I have to admit, was not unfamiliar to me, but some of the practical quirks were more surprising. I was never less than astonished, for example, at how incredibly long the bows stretched on for. At the end of any show, and whether they loved it or hated it, the audience would remain in the auditorium applauding until their hands were raw from clapping or, indeed, their voices hoarse from booing. Another tradition we don't have here is that the creative team join the actors on stage for these interminable curtain calls. It's very strange to watch director, writer and designer grinning cheerfully while the audience jeers at them with impassioned disgust.

In France, apparently, until very recently, the first day of rehearsals of a new play would begin with the playwright reading the entire play aloud from start to finish: performing all the parts, gesticulating, crying, yelling, the works. If I tried that in a British rehearsal room they'd cut me out of the email chain, move the actors to an undisclosed location and send me an invite to the opening night.

In spite of the theatre's ability to respond rapidly to social and political change, we do hold on to our traditions more tightly than we'd care to admit. It's not surprising when success or failure relies on so many uncontrollable imponderables or on the accidental alchemical reaction when audience first meets play. But let's zoom out for a moment. Making plays is a co-operative enterprise. It's what makes the theatre such a uniquely rewarding arena to work in. A company that has gathered to rehearse a play becomes a single turbo-charged brain. As writers we have to find our place inside that organism, to make our contribution and plough our particular furrow within it, so it's important to keep our eyes and ears and mind as open and receptive as possible. When we're writing for the stage we must always leave space in the work for interpretation. That's what the actors and director are required to do when they begin to work on your text. Always listen to actors. They will give you essential information about how playable the part is, how clear and credible the character's motivations, how speakable their words. Just by working on your play actors will teach you what you need and what you don't need, when you've under-written and when you've over-written: what makes sense and what is little more than gibberish.

This is one of the great, joyous advantages of being a dramatist. A novelist or a poet doesn't receive this sort of consistent feedback. The dramatist is able to adapt their voice, their style and technique as they go, to build their stage-writing muscles as they work.

In spite of this, though, every now and then in the theatre a new young writer explodes onto the scene with an electric storm of a first play. It's like a meteor crashing to earth burning tracks into the ground. A lot of people are invested in discovering the hot new thing. The danger for that person is that they can easily get swallowed in the circus that engulfs them and quickly lose their way. Arthur Miller compares these trail blazers to weeping willows: they grow upwards at a dizzying speed, wild and beautiful, making a sizzling entrance into the world, but then, rapidly, buckle under the weight of their spectacular plumage and, finally, wilt. Fading away. It's a career that has grown too fast, lacks the sinews to sustain the burning attention and withers under the strain. The oak, on the other hand, takes its time. It grows slowly, gradually, its thick stump effortlessly able to support the delicate foliage and acorns that adorn it. The oak is built to last. Better, thought Miller, to be the oak.

That is not to say we should not constantly challenge ourselves. In fact we have a duty to do so. Look at the career of Caryl Churchill time and again re-imagining the boundaries of her art. And the truth is, a playwright's career doesn't follow a linear trajectory, growing better and stronger with each play. It's a far more mixed picture. I once sat on a panel with David Hare to discuss the future of writing for the theatre and he said something that stopped me in my tracks. He said, with playwrights, there's no such thing as a career. We just go from one play to the next, that's all we *can* do. He's right. Each new play is a rebirth. You're starting from scratch. The moment you begin a new play any past successes and struggles become meaningless. All you can do is hope that you've picked something useful up along the way.

So when tradition has too tight a grip on the theatre, it becomes, to use Peter Brook's term, 'deadly'. We become in thrall to the old ways, we become drowned in our own heritage and so are doomed to repeat the same mistakes. Alternatively when the old structures are abandoned in favour of some wholly new form, our work is in danger of collapsing in on itself, of becoming pretentious or alienating or instantly out of date. This is a genuine concern in the age of cancel culture. In most areas of our life deference to past traditions hasn't just been eroded, it's been annihilated: we've become deeply suspicious of the ancient elitisms and exclusive institutions that have become so synonymous with British culture. But I'm not sure this is a particularly healthy state of affairs.

The boys I met at Eton, and of course they were all boys, were certainly not short on charm. They were engaging, intelligent, affable and self-effacing. There were about twenty in the group, all hollow cheeks and high chins and heads of flopping hair flapping at me, each more lustrously buoyant than the last. All these young men took pains to shake my hand firmly and look me directly in the eye as they did. Surprisingly, this put me immediately at ease. We took our seats and started the workshop.

I'd visited a couple of schools on my rounds that year, mostly South London comps with a diverse mix of students. Few had had much exposure to the theatre, certainly not to new playwrights. What they did have was an unencumbered access to their own creative voice. Their ideas covered a broad spectrum: they felt free to explore the limits of their imagination as well as their own experiences and anxieties. Unshackled from the heavy weight of expectation, they were able to be unashamedly themselves. Consequently, their writing was at turns messy, funny, whacky, touching, vibrant, incoherent, but always original. And that originality is the first thing a theatre is looking for in a new writer.

I usually begin these sessions by asking the students to go around the room, introduce themselves and talk about their play ideas. The Eton boys were much more familiar with the dramatic canon, but that familiarity, instead of giving them an advantage, seemed to hamstring their creative thought processes. They seemed to be measuring their ideas against the plays they'd studied, imitating an established structure that they were confident worked. They were making a fatal error. They wanted to get the right answer.

There was another thing I found curious about this first session at Eton. The boys seemed to want to pick subjects and characters that were remote from their personal experience. Perhaps they felt these subjects might be more acceptably cutting edge: council estate poverty, drug addiction, mental illness,

America ... Individually I believe these boys were no less talented or original than their South London comp counterparts, but the desire to *do well* prevented them shedding the burdens of self- consciousness and accessing their unique writer's voice. I was starting to understand what the English Master was trying to tell me. Far from being cocooned and out of touch with the prevailing culture, the Eton boys seemed, contrarily, to be acutely sensitive to their privilege, to the structures that underpin that privilege and to the perception of them in the outside world. This consistent need to engage with that world, to put oneself forward in it, to succeed at every interaction is probably an immensely useful commodity in many areas of life. Indeed, at the time of writing the UK is 'enjoying' its twentieth Eton-reared Prime Minister.

Boris Johnson, of course, has his own especial brand of shambling cynicism, something I witnessed up close when I travelled with him in a lift at the Royal Opera House. It was at the 2009 Evening Standard Theatre Awards, *Our Class* had been longlisted in a strong year (it was beaten to the nominations by *Enron*, *Punk Rock* and the eventual winner *Jerusalem*), and Johnson (then Mayor of London) was making some opening remarks. I was standing with my fellow scribe, Roy Williams, when Boris, entourage in tow, erupted into the lift in full bloviation. As the doors closed he came eye to eye with the famous and famously left-leaning Vanessa Redgrave and his jabbering intensified. 'Hello, hello, Boris Johnson,' he declared holding out his hand to her. Redgrave, iridescent in a long, slender, silvery-cream trouser suit that seemed to extend seamlessly down from her hair, took his hand curiously and, like a kind of exiled queen, moved it up and down. There then descended a deeply uncomfortable silence. The eyes of the future premier scanned the other faces in the lift for fresh meat to break the tension. They met mine, calculated with brutal efficiency that I was of absolutely no bloody use or interest, and moved on. When his gaze landed on Roy (our leading black

British playwright) he grasped his hand and said 'Ah! Now! We've met before!' 'We haven't,' Roy assured him. But Boris was locked in and he wasn't going to let a little thing like point blank denial get in the way. 'Yes, yes,' he insisted, 'we've definitely met.' If Roy was as taken aback as I was he didn't show it. 'I'm pretty sure,' he told the Mayor with heroic forbearance, 'I would remember that.' Another awkward silence. Of course, Johnson might genuinely have been convinced of the truth of this past encounter, but I could have sworn, when I met his eyes again a moment later, they twinkled as if to say: 'well, you know, worth a go.' Mercifully, the lift doors opened and we dispersed into the hall where the reception was taking place.

Politics is one thing, but when it comes to the bloodthirsty business of writing plays, we must jettison these social compulsions and drill down into the core of what makes us human: excavate our complex, clumsy and contradictory unconscious, explore how it relates to the world we're living in not how the world relates to us.

Branden Jacobs-Jenkins's firecracker of a play *Gloria* explores the question of who has the right to tell which story? The play is set initially in the offices of a New York arts magazine, but a shocking and deadly act of violence changes the characters' lives profoundly. Those who survive the carnage try to write, and then sell, their version of the event. It's a fascinating dissection of a very modern predicament: who has a moral right to which narrative? One character, that had actually vacated the office before the assault took place, still feels entitled to write about, and profit from, it. Indeed she believes her detachment from the incident gives her a broader perspective. This brings her into direct conflict with someone who *was* present and therefore believes his story *must* be the more authentic one.

Nobody deserves to tell a story any more than anyone else. Writing is an act of the imagination. Humans don't respond to the same experience in the same way or think the same things simply because they share the same background. It's absolutely essential for the playwright to assert their creative right tell any story they want: stories that might sit outside the writer's immediate frame of reference can be just as valid as those created from inside. As long there is a fidelity to the truth of our common humanity there can be no accusation of appropriation. Yes, if you have a deeper connection to the material it's possible you may write a play in a more urgent or authentic voice, but a play is not a personal lecture you will be delivering to a grateful gathering. A play is a fiction comprised of characters. And whether the character has similar attributes to you (age, gender, race, class) or is entirely different, it remains our task to climb inside the skin of someone who is *not us*. We still have to imagine their feelings and invent their commensurate behaviour. As we've seen, human beings are infinitely complicated and irreducibly distinct and so the same rules apply if we're writing about characters different to us or similar.

Writing character always requires a combination of speculation and empathy. When Euripides imagined Hecuba's howling lamentations as she held her drowned son's broken body, he wasn't simply placing words on a page; he was *living through the grief with her*. Indeed, part of the way we expand our minds and, by extension, those of our audience, is by walking in the shoes of others. We have to map our own humanity onto theirs, to conceive of how it must feel to be them, to be *that* particular person in *that* particular situation. Each time we write a character we must assume a new internal logic that might run parallel with our own or diverge from it entirely. We have to start from a new premise, assume a new set of circumstances, a new set of values. We have to open our minds, to extend ourselves in all directions, to place ourselves in the eye of the storm emotionally and intellectually or the writing will feel hollow. We must understand our characters by becoming them on the page or what we will produce will be merely an *imitation* of life, rather than life itself. We must access that part of us that can feel rage or love or vengeance or passion and report those feelings with technical, scientific and journalistic application. Finding our own creative voice allows us to move freely back and forth between these contradictions, because we always have the true north of our own creative impulse to return to. The question is: how do we locate, recognise and foster that creative voice?

I celebrate the recent efforts to bring diverse new writers to the stage. Without them the theatre can never progress or rejuvenate. But having a complex heritage or identity or even an amazing story to tell is not enough in itself to write a play. Jean Cocteau said of Victor Hugo: 'Victor Hugo is a madman who thinks he's Victor Hugo', so where does that leave us when trying to trace our own creative identity?

One night, after seeing Martin Crimp's *In The Republic of Happiness* at the Royal Court, I described him as 'the Radiohead of British playwrights'. Take a song like *Creep* or *No Surprises*. Look at how the lyrics seem to work in opposition to the melody and the musical arrangement. There's a constructive friction between the bleak nihilism laced into the lyrics and the singsong chirpiness of the tune. There's a constant argument between the accessible melody and the disruptive, jagged arrangement of it. These juxtapositions create strangely compelling and disturbing soundscapes. Crimp, in my view, does a similar thing with drama. Look at plays like *Attempts On Her Life*, *Dealing With Claire*, or *The Treatment*. There is a tension in his plays between his broken structures, his dark themes and his feather-light language that make him one of the most distinctive writers currently working in the theatre, and yet he reveals very little of himself and his background in his writing.

I, on the other hand, can't seem to escape from myself. In *Filthy Business* I wrote about the rubber shop my father ran when I was growing up. In *What We Did To Weinstein* and *The Holy Rosenbergs* and *The Glass Room* I wanted to explore competing visions of

British Jewish identity. I've always wanted to throw together characters pulled apart by ideology, but tied together by blood, because I felt both estranged from and conjoined to my own fractured tribe.

When I first met Tadeusz to start working on the English version of *Our Class*, I could tell that his initial wariness was appeased when he discovered my Jewish and Catholic ancestry. His own ideological awakening had occurred early in life as his parents, a dangerous partnership of Orthodox and Catholic, were both political prisoners and he was brought up in a post-war Poland that had not come to terms with its own complex and bloody history. In *Our Class*, an abyss is encouraged to grow between the Jewish and Catholic classmates. Classmates who felt a natural affection for and understanding of each other were prised apart by a political ideology imposed from above. The innocence of childhood was corroded by the encroachment of paranoia from a country under constant threat of invasion: Russia from the east, Germany from the west.

When I came to write the version for an English audience I had to attend to the way the characters spoke, or more specifically to the behaviour of their speech. There seemed to me, on top of the obvious religious and cultural rifts opening up between the characters, that there were also class ones. Unlike a Polish audience, a British one has been trained to see human relationships through the prism of class. It's hard-wired. The subtle modulations in how a person uses language – accent, roughness or elegance of speech, slang, phrasing, rhythm – provide clues to the character's status, attitude and destiny. It's an immediate shorthand without which, I believed, the play would have felt quite remote to a British audience. I felt it was my job to climb inside the characters and feel the bumps and smoothness of their speech, as I would do with one of my own plays. This was controversial, as Slobodzianek strikes a more neutral tone in his writing, but I felt it was necessary.

We write, consciously or otherwise, for a sort of detached, theoretical version of ourselves. There we are sitting in the audience, receiving our play. There's a famous section of the Vincente Minnelli film *An American in Paris* where Oscar Levant daydreams about conducting himself playing Gershwin's *Piano Concerto in F*. Not content with being both conductor and soloist, as the daydream deepens, he becomes all the members of the orchestra: oboist, violinist, brass, percussion. While we have to imagine the worlds and experiences and attitudes of people other than us, when it comes to things like taste and humour and emotional connection it's hard to concoct an alternative sensibility. So we use ourselves as our own weathervane. In fact we have no choice in the matter, and that should free us from any anxiety about the kind of work we think consciously that we 'should' be doing. We must write the work we are unconsciously compelled to write. That's the only way to be truthful.

This century opened with a cosmic slap in the face for our sense of security and global cohesion. Hijacked planes were flown into the Twin Towers and Western civilisation was shaken into a new consciousness. The subsequent war in Iraq was a fresh tinderbox in the Middle East, the Second Intifada raged in Israel and Palestine and our political leaders were gripped by evangelical interventionist fervour. Theatre was forced to respond.

The 1990s had seen playwrights turn inwards. Intimate plays about the atomisation of society and the splintering of conventional personal relationships had been the order of the day: plays about drug culture and self-harm and fluid sexuality and sexual incontinence among the young dominated our new play stages. Aleks Sierz's book on *In-Yer-Face Theatre* charts this period with great aplomb and my own very modest early effort, *Happy Savages*, played its fractional part, but as the world became more overtly politically aware and politicised so did playwrights.

Less than a year after 9/11, I began thinking about a play regarding this new sense I had of myself in the world. Religious and political identities were becoming crystalised and humanity seemed to the limbering up to tear itself apart. An idea came to me when I visited my ailing grandfather, Lew.

Lew, as we've seen, was a classic East End Jewish gambling, high-living socialist from The Greatest Generation. He was a committed atheist and an irredeemable humanist. He was an infinitely generous soul with a sharp sense of the absurd, but he had an acute aversion to injustice, and was quick to fly into a righteous fury if it was piqued. Bellowing down the phone at the council about the parade of incompetent "Ome 'Elps!' they'd sent him and daring them to take him to court if they ever sent him a bill became a new and enjoyable hobby. After multiple battles he got his way and received a carer he liked, Ramin. Ramin was a young Muslim refugee from the Bosnian conflict with only a smattering of English. What struck me was how these two people with very different life experiences had a natural repartee and a deep fondness for each other. On some level, I supposed, they understood that each needed the other. They would even bicker occasionally like a married couple: if my grandfather hadn't taken his pills, or if the tea wasn't made to his precise specifications.

I began to work on a two-hander set in one room about a dying man and his migrant carer. I hadn't got very far when a phone call from Jack Bradley at the National came through. He was putting together a group of playwrights with previous connections to the National Theatre Studio, but who had now scattered and were working on different things. He wanted to bring us in under the title '*Don't be a Stranger*'. The idea was that we discuss our vision for new writing in the next century. The initial group comprised writers like Tanika Gupta, Greg Burke,

Roy Williams, Richard Bean, Simon Bent, Moira Buffini, David Eldridge, Colin Teevan and Sarah Woods, and we did what any random collection of writers would do: we sat and complained. For four weeks. It was going nowhere. Along the way we lost a few writers and we gained a few writers. Then, finally, a breakthrough. We saw a play. A bad play. An old bad play. An old bad play that had a huge cast and set and had tons of money spent on it. Hang on, we thought. How come we're not putting these resources into new work? In those days the new play was expected to be a small studio space piece with a small cast in a contemporary setting and low-fi production values and a very personal theme: otherwise known as a 'me and my mates' play. Very rarely was a new writer allowed to burst forth from this orthodoxy. But the world was changing and theatre had to change with it. And so a manifesto was born. A writer's pressure group called the Monsterists. Our manifesto demanded a change in the theatre culture so that new work aspired to be big and bold, to look out rather in. We wanted to smash our way out of the black box and create state-of-the-world theatre that put event over expediency. We wanted unashamedly to return scale and spectacle to new plays and to put the country and even the world on the stage. Many plays bloomed out of this movement: Bean's *Harvest*, *England People Very Nice* and *One Man Two Guvnors*, Eldridge's *Market Boy* and *Holy Warriors*, Buffini's *Welcome to Thebes*, Rebecca Lenkiewicz's *Her Naked Skin*, Williams's *Days of Significance*, Teevan's *How Many Miles To Basra* to name a few. Many plays may not have been written since if not for this intervention.

For my own humble part, I was fired up by this new ambition of scale and I began to think of my small play on a much larger canvass. I wanted to not simply expand the play physically – cast size, setting, action – but also thematically. I wanted the play to time-travel and globe-trot and to cover themes of politics, love, death, war and literature. But how to begin?

I had my old dying man and his nurse, but how to develop this? How to connect it to my fury and confusion about what was going on in the world? One day, sitting on the stairs at the National's Studio watching the rain thrash against the long window overlooking the stairwell, I saw in my mind's eye the image of a young woman having lunch with an older man. The lunch was tense and difficult. I knew this older man was her father and that these two were deeply divided on a single issue. Israel/Palestine.

I then had the idea that the father was a literary agent and the old, dying man was his client. A writer. A socialist writer. A writer who, like the agent's daughter, also had strident views on Israel and Palestine. And maybe he had a son who took an opposite position to him. And what if the son not only took a position, but actually did something about it? What if he actually went to fight for the Israeli army? How profoundly disapproving would his father be then? In this way one idea bounced off into another and the play's structure proliferated out from there. When I sat in the 'kitchen', my airless, windowless office at the NT Studio next to the gents and wrote the scene between Josh and Yusef, a young Palestinian man he'd captured on the border after a gun battle with enemy fighters, I knew I had something explosive. The two traded jokes and clashed over the sincerity of their peoples' competing historic grievances. I knew this subject matter would deeply trouble and maybe even offend people on both sides of this intractable conflict, but the play was writing itself. It was coming to life and there was now nothing I could do to stop it. Who owns the narrative anyway?

I grew up in a Jewish enclave in North West London, but my parents were devoutly secular. My combined heritage was Polish Jews, but also Irish Catholics from Belfast, Dutch, French, possibly Iraqi (we think, it starts to get a little misty the further back you go). Even the name I inherited was fictional. My father, feeling disadvantaged and marginalised by the name Cohen, changed it a few years before I was born.

'You're a writer aren't you?' Tom Stoppard said, stalking over to me during a party at my agent's house, a note of accusation in his voice. 'Uhm … I …' I sputtered. 'Yes, yes you wrote that play, what was it?' *The Holy Rosenbergs* had just been on at the National. I took a punt. '*The Holy Rosenbergs*?' 'That's the one!' he said, then, turning to his unfeasibly glamorous wife Sabrina Guinness, he said, 'that was a big one.' Before I could ask what precisely he meant by 'big one' he demanded to know my name. When I told him he looked at me suspiciously. '*Ryan Craig*?' he repeated, then, with a hint of suspicion asked: 'Where d'you get *that* name from?' I imagined his antenna on these matters to have been sharpened by a sense of displacement from his own Jewish heritage and told him the potted history of my family moniker. He considered it, rolling it around on his tongue, 'Ryan … Craig,' concluding curiously, and possibly damningly, with: 'Good name for a writer.' Later, all puffed up with pride, I turned to my wife and said: 'See that?' She rolled her eyes. The next day I was telling my brother the story and my sister-in-law asked what we were talking about. 'Oh Ryan met Tom Stoppard last night,' he explained. 'No, no,' said my wife, a glint of mischief and mockery in her eye, 'Tom Stoppard met Ryan Craig last night.' Hubris will get you in the end. When *What We Did To Weinstein* was on at the Menier Chocolate Factory, I met Arnold Wesker. Curious to know how I'd had access to this world, he asked if I was married to a Jewish woman. When I told him I grew up in this world he was shocked. 'But your name?' he said, still dubious, 'it's so … *Celtic*'.

When I started at my secondary school, Haberdashers' Aske's, there was a large Jewish intake, so they split us up into Christian Assembly and Jewish Assembly. I started marching along after Rabbi Freeman with the other Jews. When he spotted me, this lanky kid with fair, straight hair and a stubby, piggy, little nose, he said: 'You boy. You're in the wrong group.' 'I'm not, sir', I said. 'What's your name?' he asked. 'Craig, sir', I said. 'Craig?!' His eyes narrowed as if to say don't you mock me boy. 'Craig what?' he asked finally. 'No. Craig is my surname, sir. My first name is Ryan, sir.' I could sense his exasperation building, some of my friends in the group started to snicker. '*Ryan Craig*?' the Rabbi sputtered. 'That's your name?' 'Yes sir.' 'And you say you're Jewish?' 'Yes sir.' His eyes narrowed even more. 'Are you joking?' 'No, sir.' Freeman glared at me, sizing me up. After a while he said: 'Say the *Shemah*.' Any boy who's been to Bar Mitzvah classes can recite this as second nature. 'Here o Israel the Lord our God, the Lord is One . . .' I began in my best Hebrew.

This wasn't at all strange to me. I'd always felt like an interloper, a secret agent hiding in plain sight who had to constantly justify his identity. Who was I? Where did I belong? Where had I come from? These questions are fundamental to all of us. To a writer they are meat and drink.

Remember this was the 1980s. Difference of any kind meant you were separate, strange and suspect. The term *dual heritage* was not in use and the contradictory tension in my identity became my default setting from an early age. I think any writer feels his or her own particular sense of being an outsider operating from the inside. At the interval of a new play at the Watford Palace called *Shiver* by Anglo-American writer Daniel Kanaber about the Jewish mourning period, I ran into Jack Bradley. He joked that he wasn't surprised to find me at a play about a *shivah* in North West London. 'No show without Punch', he said cheerily.

The truth is, though, I'm compelled to start a play not because I want to write about my experience, but because I have some nagging voice in my head telling me there is more to some story than everyone is prepared to admit. And because my theme is often the struggle between family, community and individual identity, the voices in my head are the voices of the fractious, disputatious people I grew up listening to. When *The Holy Rosenbergs* opened my Auntie Pauline came to an early

Saturday matinee and said afterwards: 'I knew half the audience and half of *them* I wasn't speaking to.'

When you grow up in a community you instinctively feel its pain, you celebrate its triumphs and you cringe at its shame. You understand it from the inside. If you write about it you bring that insight to the work necessarily. We have to tell the truth even if it's not what people want or expect to hear or will even accept. Tennessee Williams wrote that he wanted to give the audience 'knowledge of things that I feel I may know better that you, because my world is different from yours'. It's my belief that you reach the universal through the specific.

My mother was born less than two years after the end of the Second World War. She grew up around Petticoat Lane in peacetime London, but her attitudes and anxieties were shaped by the trauma of war and genocide. Details of the slaughter of millions of Jews began to emerge as she came into consciousness and were built into the blueprint of her mental machinery. Once, when I was a child, she spied me from her bedroom window in the front garden talking to our neighbour's grandson. She heard me ask him what his religion was. Assuming the world was split exactly evenly between Jews, Christians and Hindus, I innocently asked, 'I'm Jewish, which one are you?' At that my mother threw open her window and screamed at me to come inside. 'Never tell anyone you're Jewish.' I was five. The incident jolted me into a self-consciousness from which I've never recovered. A little later, my father's mother Dolly, in her serrated-edged Northern Irish accent carved from the grit of the Falls Road, would talk passionately about literature and language, about poetry and the saints. The horrific, violent sectarian Troubles, about which I was both fascinated and bemused, hovered silently all around us. It was forbidden to mention it. Whether explicitly or implicitly, we pass on our fears to our children, we can't help it. And once they're awoken in us, there's no going back. So when you consider that five-year-old, that child who innately understands the basic tenets of dramatic storytelling, consider this also: they know more than you think about the terrors and absurdities of the adult world.

How, then, would I answer Timberlake Wertenbaker's question today? 'If I knew then what I know now, would I ever have started as a playwright?' Honestly I'm not sure I ever really had the choice. Something conspired within me that impelled me to write. I remember being six years old and on a shopping trip with my mother. Marks and Spencer's were selling some leather-bound complete works of Shakespeare (a strange thing for them). Intrigued I heaved the enormous tome off the shelf – it was almost as big as me – and leafed through it. I saw, probably for the first time, dialogue. The words were like a claw, they reached out of the book took me by the shoulders and vigorously shook me. It was a section from *Antony and Cleopatra*. People *talking* to each other. People alive on the page.

On my twelfth birthday, my friend David Wengrow came to my house holding a slim book with a bottle green cover and a photograph of an old man picking his nose. It was a copy of Pinter's *The Caretaker*. 'We're going to read it out loud', he announced, 'I will play the brothers and you will play the tramp.' I was never the same.

I connected. The staccato language profuse with expletives and caustic humour, the simmering violence, the thrilling stillness of bodies on the brink of imminent attack, it was all so familiar to me. It reminded me so much of my East End family with their immigrant roots, piss-taking humour and inner, ironic toughness. On the back of the book was a picture of the author, a scowling man in a charcoal turtle-neck jumper. I thought: How do you become *that*?

I remember being twenty-two and sitting with my father in a local Chinese restaurant. He wanted to know what I was going to do with my life. A fair question since I'd graduated from university with a spectacularly mediocre two-two in Philosophy and History (I'd spent all my time playing in terrible rock bands and writing pretentious plays for me and my friends to star in). 'I'm going to be a playwright', I declared. He took off his spectacles and rubbed his face. He made a sort of moaning noise that I can't reproduce in words. After a moment he said. 'Why did I have you educated?' There was nothing either of us could do, the die had been cast years before, but on reflection this was a seminal moment for me. All writers need an expectation to subvert, a preconception to demolish, a fear to overcome. The creative impulse is borne out of a native friction with the world. We all need something to resist.

4 What Next? The Consequences of Resistance

A few years ago I was booed. By a whole audience. Or at least a significant enough portion of them to make it noteworthy. I was on stage taking part in a Q and A after a performance of several short plays, one of them mine, on the subject (ironically?) of censorship in the arts. We were at the now empty former offices of the *Guardian* newspaper in Farringdon (they had moved to their new glass citadel in York Way), which had been transformed into a temporary theatre space under the aegis of a group called Theatre Delicatessen. As the discussion wore on, and sensing the audience's tapering attention, Bidisha, a journalist and the chair of the panel, announced breezily, 'OK, we've got time for one more question'. A young woman in the front row posed the question she seemed to have been itching to ask all night. I was halfway through my answer to this question when the place erupted in howls of derision. What was my sin? What utterance could possibly have invited such obloquy?

I should go back. Late-ish in 2014, I was asked by a director called Cressida Brown if I'd like to contribute to a show she was making. It was to be an evening of short plays in response to a series of occasions when a UK arts institution had come under pressure to cancel or shut down various events. There's a long history of arts censorship in Britain: from the Lord Chamberlain and his blue pencil redacting anything lewd or offensive to Mrs. Whitehouse's band of moral warriors. In 1982 Whitehouse brought a private prosecution against Michael Bogdanov, the director of Howard Brenton's National Theatre play *The Romans in Britain*. The case at the Old Bailey revolved around whether a male rape scene in the play was an act of 'gross indecency'. What Mrs. Whitehouse and her lawyers were doing here was deliberately conflating the crime with its representation in art. She hadn't herself seen the play, apparently she didn't need to, to know it was what I imagine she considered unpatriotic Marxist filth, but an emissary of her organisation (the National Viewers and Listeners Association) was sitting in the back row of the Olivier (according to NT supremo Peter Hall about ninety feet from the action) and witnessed for himself the brandishing of a male appendage. No matter that one of the cast's male members was able to demonstrate in court how his own male member could be represented – by poking a finger through his trousers – the intention was still, they insisted, criminal. The case collapsed, but the crusade continued.

When Freud compares children at play to creative writers at work, he notes: 'the opposite of play is not seriousness – it is reality. For all the emotion it is charged with, the child is well able to distinguish between ... play and reality.' We have been able to tell from childhood the difference between art and real life. When we deliberately blind ourselves to these distinctions for our political ends we corrupt our own nature.

But outrage is an addictive drug. We feel mortally assaulted when someone appears to attack the things we hold sacred. We feel our identity, our very sense our selves, being fatally undermined and we'll do whatever it takes to protect it. These fights aren't just theoretical they're life and death.

In December 2004 Sikh protestors demonstrated violently outside the Birmingham Rep on the opening night of a play called *Behzti*. The playwright Gurpreet Kaur Bhatti had included a scene of rape and abuse in a Gurdwara, and has lived with the consequences ever since. The protestors felt their faith had been deeply insulted and they burned with a fury. In spite of the arts community voicing support for her freedom of speech, the theatre closed Bhatti's play after two days.

A month later, Christian groups, early adopters of the internet's power to organise, collected just shy of 50,000 signatures (the most ever at the time) demanding the BBC cancel a screening of the extravagantly 'blasphemous' *Jerry Springer The Opera*. The BBC stood firm, but the Arts Council refused to fund a tour later that year. Again the theatre community was broadly behind the creators' right to offend. Their common belief was that art was the cure, not the disease, that the freedom of the artists should take precedence over our social responsibility to any one group.

Things have changed. In 2014, The Tricycle, a theatre and cinema complex in North London, rescinded the Jewish Film Festival's invitation to show some of their programme because they were partially funded by an arm of the Israeli Government. (That summer a deadly conflict consumed Gaza and was very present in the news.) In a twist to the traditional narrative, Jewish protestors besieged the building, aggrieved that it had deprived them of art.

That same year *Exhibit B*, Brett Bailey's 'human installation' at the Barbican, saw black volunteers placed in various states of enslavement and humiliation. Bailey was white. The Barbican website claimed the work intended to chart 'the colonial histories of various European countries during the nineteenth and twentieth centuries when scientists formulated pseudo-scientific racial theories that continue to warp perceptions'. The show's critics felt this was demeaning and offensive and a cacophonous protest outside the building led to the show being shut down. Many in the arts community applauded these expurgations. They believed that social responsibility should take precedence over an individual artist's freedom of expression.

How did this reversal come about? One reading is that, like so many things, it began with Thatcher. She shattered the consensus that dominated post-war politics, promoted a rampant Darwinian monetarism and rejected the notion of a unified society. This gave way to the neo-liberal interventionist evangelism of the Blair/Brown years and in turn led to the post-crash tight-fist of the Cameron/Osborne Austerity Project. The culture reacted with a zealous austerity of its own: a moral austerity. A new sanctimony sprouted, a new social sensitivity where the intolerant would not be tolerated, and a constant and merciless micro-monitoring of language and behaviour was the order of the day. Liberalism was turned on its head. Yesterday the conservative Christian right railed against the moral incontinence of lefty artists and feckless youth, today the progressive young rail against the moral bankruptcy of the right wing media and the feckless old. In the extreme cases baby boomers born in the post-war years were branded arch-squanderers of the peace and prosperity gifted to them by the sacrifice of their parents. Not content with benefitting from free health care, affordable homes and high employment, they crashed the economy, plundered the planet, and betrayed the generations who came after them. No quarter was to be ceded in dismantling everything they cherished.

With the ascendancy of social media, anyone who feels their sensitivities unserved by the most pedestrian creative decision can send a whole organisation into spasm. 'In the absence of censorship from the outside', wrote Helen Lewis in January 2020 in a piece for *The Atlantic* magazine, touching on the National's recent run-ins over women and minorities, 'subsidised theatres are more likely to face pressure about their programming from their own tribe'.

No writer can ignore this thorough recalibration of our moral compass. No writer would *want* to ignore it. No writer would want to ignore the fact that so many of us have been awakened to inequities in our public life that have so long been neglected. A few hours ago on my TV, Black Lives Matter protestors rolled the defaced, de-pedestalled statue of a man called Edward

Colston into Bristol Harbour. This felt to many, not like a sacrilegious desecration, but an overdue reckoning. Colston had made a fortune on the backs of African slaves and his presence in bronze had long been a cause of consternation, but the council had always voted down any defenestration.

The death of George Floyd only days before had unleashed a vigilante spirit that spread like fire across America and the world and the statue was coming down whether any civic body authorised it or not. I couldn't help feeling, while I watched the protestors roll the body into river, there was something peculiarly British about this ceremonial ducking. The police, arms folded, blandly allowing the cheering, jeering crowd to go about its business, a sort of festive denuding. Even the pitching of Colston into the drink seemed somehow decorous. Of course, next, the usual parade of hired gobs filled the screens bemoaning what they call 'mob rule', an attack on history: the very same people who shamelessly deployed identity hysteria and historical blah to drag us out of Europe, mutilating fact in the process. But these dead slaver statues aren't history, they're memorials to cruelty, they're a distortion of history. They don't need a plinth. They need to be contextualised and studied so they can serve as a cautionary tale. 'Until the lion learns to write', so goes the African proverb, 'every story will glorify the hunter'. Tear them down, I say. Melt them down and make new ones: erect monuments to the immense contribution of black Britons in their place. That's living art and it doesn't deny a word of our history.

But the self-appointed Savonarolas of Cancel Culture have felt the wind at their backs recently. It's not just slavers and sex pests who are routinely excommunicated; it's anyone who doesn't fall in line with the latest orthodoxy. People are expected to parse each syllable of their public utterances for fear of unwittingly falling foul of the mob. If the most innocuous public figures can projectile the most incendiary remarks without the slightest effort, what space is left for the playwright who's supposed to be doing that for a living? How do we pick our way through this freshly laid minefield? Is it still our role to hold to account the powerful, the hypocritical, the stupid and the corrupt? Is it still our role to champion the marginalised, the silenced and the downtrodden, to be the impish thorn in the side of an unjust and judgemental system? Is it still our duty to challenge cant and falsehood, to be counter-intuitive and curious, to be obnoxious and provocative, enraging and disruptive? And when we do those things, can we still rely on our institutions to back us up?

I worry these combative instincts are being stifled. I worry that artists are self-censoring to the point of creative extinction. And that's bad news for the health of our democracy because who is left to challenge our received wisdoms and accepted morality? Who will purge and cleanse and force us to see things in new ways?

Perhaps there is some reason for hope. The Covid crisis has brought us to a fork in the road. We've been forced to pause and take a cultural inventory. What kind of theatre can we construct in the wake of this extirpation? How will we rebuild our art from the ruins of this pandemic? How will we balance social responsibility with individual free expression in this new world?

Artistic directors need to hold their nerve and put their trust in writers. Playwrights don't eat unless they're acutely alive to the shifting tensions and tolerances in our society. They inhale these sensitivities, process their inherent contradictions, and confront them head on. They've got their ears to the tarmac they can feel the future coming. They've always had to reflect on the sort of stories they could and should tell. Most playwrights I know are intensely conscious of the impact their work might have on the wider world. That's what it means to live a life stepping inside another person's skin, understanding someone separate from you, giving them a voice.

———————————————————

'He was banging his head on the desk', my mum told me over the phone one morning, her voice quailing with amazement. 'In front of everyone, you've got to see it.' Early in January 2020 an actor called Laurence Fox appeared on BBC 1's flagship political debate show *Question Time*. In response to a member of the audience's suggestion that the press coverage of Meghan Markel had racist undertones he said: 'It's so easy to throw the charge of racism at everybody and it's really starting to get boring now.' I watched through my fingers.

Fox is part of a famously patrician English acting dynasty, and it was slightly jarring to hear him speak with such authority on racism. But it's what happened next that makes this interesting. The contributor he was responding to, an academic of mixed heritage called Rachel Boyle, was having none of it. 'What bothers me about your comments', she remarked, 'is that you are a white privileged male . . .'

Ms. Boyle got no further. Half the audience shouted her down, the other half jeered in support and she was unable to develop her point (which presumably was simply that he wouldn't be able to detect an unconscious bias that is not directed against him). Fox himself emitted an extravagant groan and jack-knifed his head back with such vigour it almost flew off his neck. He swivelled his eyes back in his head, which he then flung onto the table in front of him. To some this was an act of gross insensitivity. To others it was a heroic expression of justifiable exasperation, a rejection of a reductive and prejudicial political narrative that was stifling debate.

But if all political debate is theatre and all facts up for debate, where does this leave us? It strikes me that, more and more, people seem to be detecting completely opposing meanings in precisely the same words. One part of the *Question Time* audience heard a plea for humility and enlightenment, the other an accusation: that Fox's opinion was tethered to his privilege and therefore invalid. Neither appeared remotely interested in seeing the other side. The word *debate*, which a show like *Question Time* is supposed to promote, is rendered meaningless.

'This is the modern game', Tom says in David Hare's *Skylight*, talking about the fractious relationship he has with his teenage son. 'This is men's tennis. People don't bother with rallies. You put in your big serve and you hope to hell it never comes back.'

At a time when we're culturally exiling people for the heresy of stepping outside the group, the dramatist has to embrace this danger. Where the mob tends to react as an instinctive organism, straining towards a prevailing orthodoxy, the playwright must see the other side: see through other eyes, see all the opposing views and synthesise them to find the truth: in the words of playwright James Graham, 'prosecute and defend'. If we don't do this urgently our national conversation will descend irrevocably into a carnival of resentment. 'If you don't exercise the muscle of free speech,' says Richard Bean, 'you lose it for ever.'

While the world seems to be constantly separating and segregating us, surely our response must be to insist on our similarities? Surely an insistence on how different we are simply supports the unjust structures we seek to demolish? The reason racism and sexism are such heinous aberrations is because of the truth of our common humanity. Drama exists to remind us of this truth and sharpen our sense of it. And while it's not up to the playwright to have all the answers, it *is* up to us to ask better questions. Instead of asking: are you for men or women, young or old, left or right, black or white, Brexit or Remain, masked or unmasked, why don't we ask: Are you for fairness or discrimination? Justice or inequity? Pluralism or tribalism? Truth or lies?

But putting anything into the public domain today is like catching a falling knife. Outrage is the new high of choice, but it's a sugar rush, it won't sustain us in a time of crisis. What we need is a deep and considered rage. Rage that's been simmering away for years, for decades, rage that's been nourished by lived experience and the agony of consciousness.

Late in 2005 I read about David Irving's arrest and imprisonment in Austria under a law that made denying the Holocaust a crime. At the same time there was some discussion in the UK that the Blair government was considering a similar law. I told Anthony Clark at the Hampstead Theatre I wanted to write about this and he commissioned the play that eventually became *The Glass Room*. I didn't want to write about Irving himself: I wasn't interested in his story or what motivated him, but I was interested in how you could test the limits of free speech. I was also intrigued by the psychology that drove intelligent human beings to become immune to facts. It wasn't a huge stretch then for me to imagine a law proscribing Holocaust denial had been introduced in Britain and I invented a female academic called Elena Manion who was being tried for breeching this law. I placed Elena in a safe house in a London suburb because she had been receiving death threats and gave her an idealistic half-Jewish lawyer to prep her for an imminent trial. I reckoned, this way, I could contain the drama in a pressure-cooker environment and then turn up the heat when the lawyer felt caught between his personal integrity and his professional duty.

I was so enthused by the neat construct I'd concocted and the burning urgency of the subject, I completely ignored the fact that the play was likely to annoy and upset pretty much everyone. My energies were too focused on climbing inside the skin of someone who thought, at least on one particular subject, as differently to me as it was possible to imagine. I wanted to understand the mechanics of that thinking: What would compel this woman – educated, urbane, successful – to risk her freedom and her career over something as repellent as denying the existence of the gas chambers? What would drive her to try to reason away, in the face of such overwhelming evidence, the murder of six million people?

In my first year at Leeds University I was browsing the Brotherton Library when a title caught my eye: *Das Judenthum in Der Musik*. It was by Richard Wagner, whose music ensorcelled me. I took the book out and read it later that afternoon. I couldn't believe my eyes. The pages sputtered with a venomous hate I wasn't expecting.

I was aware he had some questionable views, but I wasn't prepared for this feral assault on 'Jewishness'. He attacked composers like Meyerbeer and Mendelssohn, wildly successful at the time, and Jews in general, for contaminating German culture. I put the book on the shelf in my room and made an executive decision: this hideous polemical bile is not going back to that library.

This 'stand' quickly turned into a mini war between the library and me. I was threatened with a large fine and maybe even a prosecution. I was told I couldn't take any other books out until I'd returned the Wagner. I was unmoved. I was a bolshie nineteen-year-old with a cause and I was perfectly ready to die on this hill, I was ready to take whatever they threw at me, I wasn't backing down. 'Do your worst Brotherton Library. I speak for my people'.

This was 1991, so it was a very private war. I didn't publicise my protest, I had no online petitions to rally the troops or echo my outrage, I only had myself and my conscience. I considered destroying the book. I remember sitting in my room looking at the thing, turning it over in my hand. There's something about a book, its fragility and tangibility, the way the pages oxidise over time, yellowing and changing, the aromatic mustiness it acquires, the way the spine cracks and clicks with use: it's a living thing. Even its objectionable contents evolve their meaning and potency as their context changes. Even the words I'm writing now may trigger different resonances in a month, a year, a decade's time.

My grandmother Dolly always treasured her books. She grew up on the Falls Road in a working-class Catholic family with a brace of siblings. Belfast was roiling with violent sectarianism and she would disappear into books, consoled and elevated by them. 'I want a writer in the family', she'd instruct me when I was a boy, in that corrugated Ulster accent, her words somehow laced with threat. (Actually she got two writers when my brother Dean went to Hollywood and he too looted our family identities for films like *Death at a Funeral*.) With Dolly in mind, how could I destroy this book? It had opened my eyes to an especial acrimony in the world I hadn't previously appreciated. It had informed me. Armed me.

No artist is more cancellable than Richard Wagner. His values, even for his day, were repellent: apart from being overtly racist he was, by all accounts, disloyal and deeply unpleasant. But his music stirs the soul. The great musician Daniel Barenboim insists on playing Wagner in Israel and in the occupied territories. He takes ownership of the work and therefore of its meaning. Clive James, when asked how to get more young people into poetry, said 'ban it'. Drive something underground and it acquires a dark, mythic power. Tolerate it, interpret it, contextualise it and take ownership of it and you harness that power for good.

After a few months of my Mexican stand off, I marched Wagner back to the library. 'Here's your book', I said haughtily. 'And I've certainly no intention of paying any fines.' Then I marched out. I never heard another word on the matter.

The subjects of your plays choose you not the other way around. They light a fire somewhere near your solar plexus and insist on being brought to life. They care nothing for the trouble they may cause you: they yearn to live and they won't go quietly. You midwife them into existence or you die a little inside. Writers who ignore these yearnings to avoid causing offence or inviting opprobrium will feel their hearts shrivel, become gangrenous, and die.

The Glass Room was only my second grown-up play, so the process of writing was also a process of figuring out my own thoughts and feelings: How do we represent highly contentious figures on stage? How do we balance their right to speak with the damage they can do? How long do we leave a dangerous and hateful lie suspended in space before we cut it down?

I was born in an NHS maternity hospital (now defunct) about two hundreds yards up the road from where the Hampstead Theatre now stands. I spent the first two years of my life in a poky ground floor flat in Hendon off the North Circular, before my brother Dean arrived and we moved to a semi in Mill Hill. It's a strange place Mill Hill. It exists in a sort of nowhere space. Not town, not country. The busy Broadway curves through the residences like a toothsome grin. The even busier Roundabout loops traffic in and out of London, north and south and west and east in from Mill Hill Village and back to the Broadway. David Hare believes a lower-middle-class suburban upbringing is the perfect breeding ground for a writer. Maybe.

My late teen hunting ground was the pubs and delis and late-night pancake bars and bagel bars around Golders Green and Hampstead and Belsize Park. I've had two plays on the main stage at Hampstead and each time it's felt like streaking naked through my old neighbourhood. On the first Saturday preview of *The Glass Room* there was a palpable febrility in the air. The house was full, they were hanging from the rafters. The predominantly Jewish audience had come with gritted teeth: as if we were actually putting a real live denier on stage. It felt like a political rally, not a new play. When Siân Thomas, playing Elena, stepped on to the stage she was met with a gasp of hostility, a physical wave of repulsion: you could taste it. The whole theatre hummed with rage.

As the play progressed and we watched Elena's malignant apologia challenged with facts and evidence, the tension abated, but only a little. If you do your job properly and put living breathing people on stage, you shouldn't complain when the audience conflates the fiction with the fact. In the bar after the show, the cast, director and myself decided to be very open to receiving feedback. I remember standing in the theatre bar with the irreplaceable Fred Ridgeway who'd played Pete Brody, the Jewish lawyer's father, speaking to a real Holocaust survivor and her family. Only now, writing these words, do I really appreciate how brave it was for that woman to even sit through my play, let alone approach us afterwards. To revisit the hell she must have gone through. I now appreciate that she knew she *had* to confront this horror again. That such things can never be airbrushed out of history because we find them distasteful. They must be confronted because the past is always alive and informing the present.

'The truth emerges', says Oskar Eustis, director of the Public Theater in New York, 'in the conflict of different points of view'. Eustis believes democracy and drama are co-dependent, both rising from the roots of society, one feeding the other. A healthy democracy has a vibrant and confident theatre. A good play has dialogue consisting of the exchange of opposing ideas making the drama live because it's at once active and reactive. This Socratic ambidexterity is crucial in playwriting and the only way to get to grips with the great issues of our day. In fact this approach is employed in two of the best American plays of the last few years. Lynn Nottage's *Sweat* is set in a seedy bar in a dying steel town. The plot centres on a parole officer and her two childhood friends, and shows how racial tensions that lay dormant during times of prosperity, rise to the surface when things get tough. Without judging, the author allows the characters to thrash around freely expressing their rage, resentments, and desires. In J.T. Rogers's play *Oslo*, a real-life Norwegian couple, both diplomats, hatch a plan to yoke together opposing parties in the Israel/Palestine conflict at a remote retreat and attempt the 'impossible': to broker a peace deal. After a frosty start, the old enemies eat, sing, reminisce, trade jokes, tell stories about their families, and, slowly, surely, begin to see each other as human beings. It sounds idealistic, but it never feels naïve, because it reveals a truth: when we see people as no more than representative symbols, there's conflict. When we see them as human, with the same dreams and fears as us, there's hope.

This doesn't mean that the stage is a cosy, happy-clappy, love-fest. No. The stage is a bear-pit. It's not a safe space but a cauldron. A crucible of violence and hate, lust and envy: a place to deconstruct all the darkness in the human soul and bring us to enlightenment. It's a place of constant intellectual and emotional risk. It's no wonder we so often trip and fall and get eaten alive. But we get up and do it again. 'There is no escape', the dancer Rudolf Nureyev once told the *New York Times*, 'really what it boils down to is that we are paid for our fear'.

I learned on *The Glass Room* that however cerebral and considered your text, the theatre is a visceral medium. The audience receives the play, not with their head, but with their gut. Consider that when you send your actors into that bear-pit. They are ambassadors for the emotions of the drama as much as they are dispensers of the arguments: the more controversial the subject the heavier that emotional burden weighs on them. Before the first performance of *The Holy Rosenbergs*, I found Henry Goodman prowling panther-like around the circular set, breathing in the house before the kill. The role of David Rosenberg was remarkably close to him in age and background and for an actor who likes to construct his characters so meticulously from within this must have felt deeply exposing. As the audience gathered in the foyer I went over to ask if he was OK. He met my eye with that steely glare of his and said in a low growl: 'I've never felt so naked.'

I've written overtly about my identity for twenty-plus years: I exist, like any writer I know, in every character, and in every line of my plays. I've used these characters to explore the darker parts of myself. 'Sometimes a writer has to smash the mirror', wrote Pinter, 'it is on the other side of that mirror that the truth stares at us'. I've tried to use the stage to work out the most intractable problems I can think of in the most public space possible. Looking back I realise I seem to have devised a way to set myself up to consistently fail. Over and over I've opened myself to exposure, mockery, derision and dismissal, yet I keep going back. Why?

We are, like our art, flawed and flailing: we're works in progress. Plato tells us, in the physical world, there's no perfect table only a table that resembles or even imitates the 'ideal table' of our imagination. With plays, the more we aspire to the ideal, the more we open ourselves to criticism and the harder we fall when we fail.

Always listen to those who've failed the most. They'll have learned the hard way and they have the most wisdom to impart. Never love an artist who's never been massacred by the critics. A writer who's pleased everyone and offended no-one has risked nothing. Has changed nothing. 'To be a good human being', says the philosopher Martha Nussbaum, 'is to have a kind of openness to the world. An ability to trust uncertain things beyond your own control that can lead you to be shattered.... To be morally destroyed'. The ethical life must be based, she says, on a trust in the uncertain, on 'a willingness to be exposed'. Without this we cannot make art.

In 2013 I met the playwright Howard Brenton when we were working on a youth project for the National Theatre. When I met him he told me he'd seen my film *Saddam's Tribe* and particularly enjoyed the scene with the father and the son, when Saddam tells Uday he's an embarrassment. The scene, brilliantly played by Stanley Townsend and Danny Mays (today we'd insist on more ethnically accurate casting, though that doesn't negate their professionalism), shows Saddam discovering Uday has shot the Minister of the Interior, his own uncle, over a snub to a party. He yells at his son, thrashing him in front of the palace guards. When I finished the first version, I was exhilarated. I'd filled the scene with classical references and clever comebacks and furtive looks and loaded subtext, but when I turned on the computer the next day it was gone. The whole scene wiped. All that work! I got that belly-stabbing feeling you do when you realise technology (or more accurately your own ineptitude) has thwarted you again. I had to deliver the script that afternoon so I had no choice but to hunker down and write the scene over. I couldn't remember any of the clever stuff, just the basic outline. He's furious about his son embarrassing him. The son begs for forgiveness, insisting he's the creature his father made him. The new scene was, by necessity, bald, brutally direct and lit with fury. I thanked Howard for liking the scene and told him the whole thing was an accident: the result of a desperate salvage operation. He shrugged and said: 'Of course.' Drama is emotion. When you strip out the fat and head for the marrow, then you've got something.

Saddam's Tribe was shot over about six weeks in the autumn of 2006 and I spent that time bouncing between rehearsals in Hampstead for *The Glass Room* and the shoot in West London (a disused carpet warehouse in Neasden doubling for Saddam's palace in Baghdad). When everything was up and running I took a break for a few days in the Cotswolds. A day or so in I was phoned up by the Hampstead press officer asking me to come back to London immediately: David Irving had been released from prison. He was on his way back to the UK and *BBC News At Ten* wanted to interview us both.

One of the many contradictions in being a playwright is that we spend the bulk of our time in quiet obscurity and secret toil, and then the play's on, the circus is in town and the writer's wheeled around like a show pony. But this interview troubled me. I was conflicted. While it's the writer's job to be an advocate for our work, this play wasn't about Irving. But then how could I write a play about free speech and then refuse an invitation to discuss it? In the end a biblical fog swept over Europe, closed the roads into London and grounded Irving's plane in Vienna. The interview was off: censored by an act of God.

A few years later I was in the audience at the Olivier Theatre to see a Q and A with the playwright Richard Bean, when the stage was stormed. We'd been expecting trouble. Bean's play *England People Very Nice* provoked lashing indignation for 'stereotyping' migrant communities. But Richard intended to satirise the racism these communities encountered, not reinforce it. The play's repeating structure and cartoonish style exists to reveal how each new wave (French Huguenot, Irish, Jewish, Bangladeshi) similarly confronts ignorance, insults and fear from the local population, before settling, innovating and moving on. The author's intention was to throw his arms open in a great cry of welcome. (He consulted me while he was writing the Jewish section, but I don't think I was very helpful, I just advised him to read Adam Biro's *Two Jews On A Train*.) Though the joke was meant to be on the abusers not the abused, as is increasingly the case, the two became conflated.

Theatre's a blood sport. Your intentions may be pure, but when you give a character the flesh of life the audience reacts instinctively to that life. The concepts and ironies of the play get lost in the heat and grit of performance. The ideas only begin their work in the minds of the audience long *after* they've left the auditorium. That's because a play is the beginning of the conversation not the end. It exists to probe and explore: to be an opening up not a shutting down.

'I absolutely accepted', Bean said later, 'that I would be criticised for representing those communities', but goes on to say that it's not only reductive but unfeasible to limit a writer only to stories about their own background. When his play about the Hull trawler-men he knew as a child, *Under The Whaleback*, was produced in his hometown, Bean was criticised because he was born in the wrong part of the city. How could he write about people from west Hull, when he's from *east*?

'Any time you represent any community', says Bean, 'you're up for it. Because the writer is never, and I mean *never*, going to be part of that community because *they are a writer . . .*'

Traditionally, though, and frustratingly, work that emerges from an immigrant community has been considered niche in this country. Their voices have been marginalised, relegated to the fringes and the smaller spaces. This is changing, but slowly. In Aleks Sierz's book about new plays in the first decade of this century, *Rewriting the Nation*, he writes of the death of ideology and how in these times it is 'our aesthetics' that are 'our identity'. But in the last few years, theatres have worked hard to open their spaces to a broader diversity of voices with the confidence to talk about their backgrounds. These voices, by reaching out from their communities, rather than being confined to them, will redefine what it means to be British.

A writer is always outside society looking in and always inside their identity looking out. So often there's a missed connection between how we see ourselves and who we really are. The writer has to tear away the screen and show us our true selves, to 'smash the mirror', even if it's antagonistic to do so.

In his book *Shakespeare: The Invention of the Human*, Harold Bloom makes the bold assertion that it is a playwright, in this case Shakespeare, who created our very perception of what it is to be human. Before him, character was destiny and destiny was determined by the gods. A human life had an inevitable trajectory and their flaws were singular, fatal and unavoidable. Shakespeare synthesised these ideas, refining them and enhancing them by adding complex dimensions. He didn't use these terms, but his characters were deepened and defined by identity, psychology, circumstance and individual choice. How thrilling must it have been for those early audiences to see *Hamlet*: so multidimensional, so unpredictable, so *human*.

'In Shakespeare', writes Bloom, 'characters develop rather than unfold, and they develop because they reconceive themselves. Sometimes this comes about because they *overhear* themselves talking ... Self-overhearing is the road to individuation.' Shakespeare was writing at a time of public health emergencies, massive social upheaval, widespread censorship and political terror, but his imagination seems endlessly liberated and his theatre unbounded. He co-opted Greek mythology and recent history and contemporary texts and scripture, then broke, or changed, or adapted Aristotelian laws as he saw fit. He appropriated at will, used what he wanted, discarded what he didn't, embraced tradition and unbuckled himself from it at the same time: he threw off the orthodoxy of the day and the world was never the same.

But Shakespeare wasn't a god or a prophet, just a bloody good artist. If we are going to build a new theatre for a new nation, we need to step out of his shadow and find our own creative confidence. We need to take a leaf out of his playbook and liberate ourselves. Shakespeare's plays aren't perfect things; actually, they're gloriously *im*perfect things, that's what makes them so messily, chaotically human. They're often badly plotted, and full of contradictions and eccentricities, but they teem with life and that's why they survive.

Dr Johnson attributed Shakespeare's eminence to the diversity of his characters. Bloom agrees. 'No-one', he argues, 'before or since Shakespeare, made so many separate selves'. This is, I think, why Shakespeare is constantly being reinterpreted, constantly being made relevant, constantly being brought into the present tense: from Brook's *Dream* to Tim Supple's astonishing 2006 Indian *Dream*; from Orson Welles's 1936 all-black *Macbeth* to Gregory Doran's all-black *Julius Caesar*; from Kathryn Hunter's Lear to Harriet Walter's Brutus. The plays withstand these mutations, indeed are enhanced by them, because they are about the fundamental universality of human experience. Shakespeare seemed to understand our psychology in such a comprehensive way; the plays were so specifically *about* who we are at bottom, about why we behaved the way we behaved, about the persistence of our natures in the face of extreme challenges, that they not only reach out across time, but across gender and identity. In fact Shakespeare was highly partial to a bit of gender swapping, his characters so often identity shape-shifters. I remember watching Piers Morgan on morning telly apoplectic about the BBC insisting there were now a *hundred* genders. I'm sure, if Shakespeare were alive today, he'd think: 'Really? That few?'

In 2015 a production of *Hamlet* with Benedict Cumberbatch caused outrage when its director Lyndsey Turner had the temerity to move the 'To be or not to be' soliloquy to the beginning. 'Indefensible!' cried *The Times* after seeing a preview. Why? Why this hysteria? Why this purism? When Thomas Ostermeier moved the same speech all over the shop in his production, no-one batted an eyelid. Is that because he's German? Do we expect a separate moral standard from British directors? Must they observe some special cultural reverence?

Nonsense. Shakespeare's plays will survive these directorial flourishes as they will survive every other free interpretation. I'd go further and say they survive *because* of these artistic freedoms. They are not museum pieces carved in bronze and fixed forever: they are living art. Since Peter Brook's gravity defying *Midsummer Night's Dream* in 1970, Shakespeare's popularity has grown not dwindled. We must be as free with our expression as those artists are with his.

I regretted accepting the job (from Cressida Brown) the moment I hung up the phone. A five-minute play about censorship in the arts? Is she mad? What the hell can I write about censorship in five minutes? It might as well be five hours.

Withering into a husk of self-doubt and panic I started to cast around for an idea: if there's no idea, there's no play. It seemed impossible to squeeze so massive a subject into so microscopic a framework. It's no accident, I think, that, as he aged, Beckett's work progressively shrank: he wasn't getting more indolent, he was getting more ruthless: distilling his metaphors into concise poetic slivers. Harold Pinter and Caryl Churchill are the only other playwrights I can think of who've followed a similar trajectory of attenuation and Churchill was penning her own five-minuter as part of our show. No pressure then.

I naturally over-write. My plays can quickly become verbose and flatulent so a lot of the graft is paring down, jettisoning the unnecessary guff. With a five-minute play I'd have even more winnowing to do than usual. I had a pretty incendiary idea for a comic drama about a Jewish circumcision ceremony – the baby's parents decide it's inappropriate in the modern world, but the grandmother, believing it is an essential part of his identity, kidnaps the baby and has him shorn in secret. As soon as I started giving voice to the characters the text ballooned into a swollen, misshapen mess. Five minutes? This was madness.

The deadline day arrived and I had nothing. I decided I'd ring Cressida to tell her it was impossible, I couldn't do it, we were too close to the wire, I give up. Before I did I took the dog for a walk. Maybe the endorphins'll kick in, those BDNF proteins'll do their work. Halfway across Wandsworth Common an image appeared in my mind. A man walks on to a stage. Pre-curtain. Middle-aged, middle-class, frayed suit, put-upon, rictus grin and stewing with anger, impotency and regret. He welcomes the audience to the theatre and launches into an elaborate apology. For various reasons the play they've gathered to see has been cancelled. This was it! I don't have to write the play about circumcision, I just have to have someone say I did and that it's been censored. The monologue would essentially be a list of all the reasons the management had felt it inappropriate to present the piece. From the computer it was written on to the inflammatory subject matter to the refusal of the playwright to redact or change a single word. At the same time this theatre manager is unspooling before our eyes, his apology soon mutating into the flagellating tirade of a person suffering a painful and public nervous breakdown.

I bolted back home with Monty (my cocker spaniel), grabbed my laptop and dashed to the local noodle bar to write the thing before it flew out of my head. Like a torrent this man's voice flowed out, full of frustration and confusion, caught between defending his theatre's reputation and protecting the freedom of his artist. I titled the play *Please Forgive Us Whoever You Are* and sent it off. Cressida seemed happy and she threw it into the mix. (This nano-play has since been presented in London, Edinburgh, New York and Paris.)

Then the calendar turned and a new year was upon us. 2015 was only seven days old when the world of politics and art collided in the most shocking fashion. On the 7th of January on the Rue Nicolas-Appert in the 11th arrondissement of Paris two brothers armed themselves with deadly weapons, forced their way into the offices of a small satirical magazine and started the killing. In the ensuing melee seventeen people lost their lives and eleven were injured. The brothers were responding to a cartoon they found offensive.

The *Charlie Hebdo* attack stirred a wave of global outrage and an all too brief moment of universal solidarity. It was in this context we were presenting our plays about censorship in the arts. *Walking The Tightrope*, as it was now called (a prescient title if ever I heard one), ran to good and appreciative houses and received pretty warm reviews too: a frisson of press excitement was created by Neil Labute's offering, which was a deliberately noxious little grenade about race and anal sex. The presence of other luminaries – Caryl Churchill, Mark Ravenhill, April De Angelis, Hattie Naylor, Hannah Khalil, Tim Fountain, Julia Pascal, Evan Placey, Gbolahan Obisesan and Sarah Solemani – gave the whole enterprise heft and traction and Cressida and I were even invited on to Radio Four's flagship arts show *Front Row*. (To be quizzed with quicksilver professionalism and thoroughness by the music journalist John Wilson, of whom we were all jealous as he was heading straight after us to interview PJ Harvey.) We comported ourselves, in my view, reasonably well and everything was going fine with the show when Cressida asked me to take part in a Q and A panel discussion after one of the performances. 'Sure', I thought, 'what could possibly go wrong?'

The show that night, I thought, played to an unusually muted response. Afterwards, I was introduced to my fellow panellists: the mediator Bidisha and Natalia Koliada, a director of the Belarus Free Theatre. Both were completely delightful. Three chairs were set on the stage facing the audience in adversarial anticipation. I noticed as soon as I sat on mine the crowd was twitchy. Their blood was up, something about the show had riled them (this, after all, was partially the point), but I decided to pick my way through my answers carefully. We fielded questions of censorship, taste, satire and violence without too much resistance then, wrapping it up, Bidisha asked for a final question. A young woman in the front row raised her hand. She asked: 'who is this show for?'

Pretty much every panel I've ever been on someone asks a question like this. It bothers me, I can't help it. What's the subtext to this question? What's it implying? That some people deserve theatre more than others? That writers should write for one group and not another? I don't know any working playwright worth their salt who only wants to speak to one tribe. All of us want as diverse a group of people as possible, because our job is to connect to some universal truth about the human condition. We don't stand on the door like nightclub bouncers checking everyone's wearing the right ideological trousers.

I turned to Bidisha and with misplaced confidence declared that I could take this one. 'We have to accept', I began, 'that at this point the theatre is broadly a middle class pursuit...'

That's as far as I got. Possibly learning from my mother, I'd intended to use this sweeping stinger as a hook to grab the audience's waning attention. I intended to launch, thereafter, into a devastating disquisition on the Greeks and their infant democracy and their public play competitions segueing to the dominating influence of the groundlings on the Elizabethan theatre and the Bowdlerising of Shakespeare's text that appealed so perfectly to the puritan Victorian mentality that they'd embraced censorship with such alacrity they nearly strangled the life out of our greatest dramatist. Then I'd round off with how the culture had been hijacked and weaponised in the political class struggle of the twentieth century, concluding with a lip-quivering flourish that we must reclaim the theatre as a classless art form.

I didn't get to say any of that. The phrase 'middle class' had so potently triggered the (almost exclusively middle class) audience and driven them into a convulsion of disgust, they just started braying at me. A young man shouted over the din: 'you can't say that!' Brazenly eschewing the theme of the evening; or perhaps embracing it?

Looking back I can see the fault, dear reader, was, in some part, my own. Though it certainly wasn't my intention, I must have sounded like a cynical and dismissive tool. I appeared to diminish the issue and the questioner by reducing them both to a label. But what is more important for our purposes is this: I had blundered blindly into the new world order. The audience were as much offended by my words as the fact that they were being ejaculated from a mouth that belonged to someone white, male, and middle-class.

'The theatre and arts world', wrote the journalist Sagal Mohammed in a 3 December 2019 article about Jackie Sibblies Drury's Pulitzer Prize-winning play *Fairview* for *AnOther*, 'is traditionally dominated by the white middle class. Last year *The Guardian* reported a Warwick Commission's 2015 document found that "the wealthiest, best educated and least ethnically diverse eight per cent of the population were still the most 'culturally active"' in the country'.

'There are all sorts of social codings in theatre', the article reports Sibblies Drury saying, 'things that tell people that they're not invited and that they shouldn't come. It's like if you walk passed [*sic*] a very fancy coffee shop in a gentrified neighbourhood. It's not telling the people that lived there originally not to come inside but there's something about the flat-white latte cup that makes people feel like they're uninvited and that it is economically priced out for them, and they would be made to feel uncomfortable in that space. So in theatre, there are people who are trying really hard to undo that but it's a process.' Everyone who works in theatre knows its survival and vitality depends on encouraging a younger, wider, more diverse audience. Why has it been so slow to change?

In *The Smoking Diaries* the playwright Simon Gray writes about a long career that began in the late 1960s. In it he complains that 'a number of critics have sneered at my typical English middle class, public school and university educated, literary, so forth, so forth …'. How many of those early critics, I wonder, were also public school, university educated, middle class literary, and so on and so forth themselves? Close to 100 per cent? Why this self-suspicion?

After my gaffe elicited hoots of derision my fellow panellist Natalia Koliada came to my rescue: 'The thing about this country', she told the audience, 'is that you don't understand the importance of freedom of expression because it's never been taken away from you.'

If we so often define ourselves in opposition to something, perhaps, after so many years of prosperity and influence, the British middle classes have landed at a point where the only opposition to their identity has had to come from within.

Tamsin Oglesby's Old Vic play *Future Conditional* follows Alia, a young Hazara girl from the Pakistan/Afghanistan border who is educated in England. Confronted with the strange concept of fee paying private schools being called public schools, she says: 'That's what I like about your language. One word means two contradictory things. Is how you avoid fundamentalism.'

We'll never get to the root of British identity until we accept the contradictions at the heart of our language and culture. We'll never truly change and progress until we embrace our own reality. The writer's task is to present that reality to us, to draw us in, hold our attention and force us to hear things about ourselves we might find unpalatable.

My dad grew up in Hackney and worked on the East End markets. His family of rubber merchants were stallholders before they were shop owners but that 'market mentality', as they called it, never left them. My father, though, came of age in 'swinging' 1960s London and wanted to cater to changing tastes in design and individualism. He stocked futons and beanbags and gaudy cushions cut to any size, but the Holloway Road community stubbornly refused to change at the same rate as his vision. Unable to accept that reality and adapt his thinking, his business struggled. My childhood is pocked by the endless existential anxieties over that shop and his livelihood.

I used to write in a cheap and cheerful little café run by a Greek-Cypriot family who'd been in our neighbourhood for decades. Over the last few years the area has undergone a rapacious gentrification and the café closed. In its place, a dynamic triumvirate of young, trendy avocado-smashers moved in, stripped out the twee furniture, turbocharged the menu and hit the ground running. They knew exactly what their customers wanted and their coffee was the best around. Consequently every weekend the road outside suddenly heaved with the professional brunch crowd. I remember coming out of the café one day with my takeaway coffee and bumping into an older neighbour of ours. 'You don't go there do you?' he huffed. 'Yes', I said, confused, 'why?' 'I don't trust it', he said shaking his head suspiciously. 'Funny smell. Foreign muck.' I realised later that it was he who felt like the foreigner. He who felt excluded. He who felt suddenly alien in the place he'd lived his whole life. He could not adapt.

My mother reached upwards from where she started and took my father with her. They were working-class East End kids who saw being part of the English middle classes as a wholly positive aspiration. They thought it would make them healthier, safer, and more accepted. They thought it would give their children opportunities they never had. They changed their tastes accordingly, moved to areas they considered 'on the up', and sent their boys to the 'right' schools. When they achieved 'middle class-ness' they became (marginally, but still) more socially and culturally progressive. They felt confident enough in their new status to take us to 'the theatre'. They took us to pantos with people like Jim Davidson and Lionel Blair, and musicals with David Essex. My grandfather Lew was able to score tickets from his mate who became a theatre angel and we graduated to West End plays like Richard Harris's *The Business of Murder* with Richard Todd at the Savoy, and Bernard Slade's *Fatal Attraction* with Susannah York and Denis Quilley. Front row seats for *Antony and Cleopatra* with Vanessa Redgrave and Timothy Dalton was memorable. I was mesmerised by all of it.

Change happens between generations and within classes and hidden codes beam out in all directions. If you used the words 'middle class' and 'privilege' as sticks with which to beat my parents they'd look at you as if you were mad. They worked their whole lives to be those things, for their children to have that status. If we want the theatre to ooze a little less with white middle-class privilege we have to radically change our aesthetic values, change what we project to the world. Are we prepared to do that?

The local market where we live has changed beyond recognition from when we moved here only ten years ago. The fishmongers and greasy spoons moved out and the artisan bakers and vegan restaurants moved in. When the halal butcher on the corner was evicted his sons turned the premises into a mobile phone repair centre. I remember sitting outside one of the busy cafés on a warm spring day and saw a workman in a hi-vis vest walk up and study the menu. Hunger pinching his cheeks, he shook his head in despair. He was about to walk away, but decided to stand his ground. In a desperate appeal, he stood before us, opened his arms in a strangely theatrical gesture and, his voice cracking with desperation, cried: 'I just want a bacon sandwich. That's all. Where can I get just a plain, white bread, bacon sandwich!?' Our heads must have shot up like surprised gazelles. We looked at him with startled curiosity as if he were speaking an alien language.

Are we really this far gone? Should a taste for white-bread bacon sandwiches really divide us so definitively from each other? Theatre should and can speak to everyone because it's *about* everyone. But it's still the case that the latte-drinking middle class professionals hanging outside my local café are much more likely to see *Fairview* at the Young Vic than my neighbour or the man in the hi-vis vest. And their middle-class parents are likely to go to most of the other theatres. You can't fix a problem until you can look it honestly in the face.

In Reni Eddo-Lodge's volcanic and hugely influential book *Why I'm No Longer Talking To White People About Race*, the author notes with irony that since writing a blog of the same name, 'I now spend most of my time talking to white people about race.' One of the most searching sections of the book is when she interviews the leader of the BNP. This curiosity about what connects us to even our most extreme opposites is crucial if we are to shift the culture and break the identity stasis. Our humanity is the same at its core whether we're separated by gender or race or political affiliation or even whether we're divided by centuries. We have as much in common with the characters of Aeschylus and Shakespeare as we have with those of most contemporary playwrights: it's why they're still relevant, why they still speak to us, because they capture something universal about what it is to be human.

My first TV script-writing job was with a now defunct Channel 5 soap called *Family Affairs*. Any continuing TV drama is a factory line, each show with its own internal machinery. On *Family Affairs* a team of story-liners would thrash out a beat-by-beat document. This consisted of a couple of explanatory paragraphs for each scene of the half-hour. This would be biked over to the writer (no email attachments in those days) and the writer would translate this document into a shooting script: dialogue, characterisation, stage direction etc ... then hand it on to the production team. One day, I was reading through my beat-by-beat for the coveted Friday episode. (We all wanted the Friday because it was the culmination of the week's stories and contained all the action and none of the set-up.) I noticed, reading, that one of the stories was remarkably similar to the plot of Euripides' *Hippolytus*. A distinguished GP had left his wife for his young secretary who in turn fell in love with the GP's teenage son. This had shades of the tragedy of Theseus, Phaedra and Hippolytus. A couple of thousand years after Euripides wrote his masterpiece the themes of filial loyalty, moral shame and irrepressible lust were clearly as relevant to the broad human experience as ever.

I tried to layer some coded references to the ancient Greeks into my script as a nod to anyone else out there in TV land who might make the same connection, but this was unappreciated by management: 'Our audience don't know who Euripides is,' I was told. 'If one person knows, it'll surely be worth it', was my naïve response. I was not invited to write more episodes.

'The cataclysm has happened', wrote D.H. Lawrence in the years after the First World War, 'we are among the ruins, we start to build up new little habitats, to have new little hopes: there is now no smooth road into the future: but we go round, or scramble over the obstacles.' After the scorched earth devastation of the Coronavirus pandemic, theatre finds itself fighting for its life. We can't and mustn't take its survival for granted. We have to reach out in ways we never dreamed. To do this we have to put our trust in our writers. A new play can define a moment in time. It can speak urgently to us through characters that teem with inner life. It can bring people together from all generations and backgrounds in common accord.

The leaders of even our most ideologically driven institutions are now battling for theatre's post-Covid survival by publicly emphasising its broad appeal, its mainstream popularity. They've pointed, rightly, to the vast audiences (surpassing those attending football matches). They've pointed, rightly, to the fact that every pound spent in art subsidy is returned five-fold in taxes to the state coffers. They've pointed, rightly, to the multitude of international artists of stature, suckled on the British stage, that go on to have stellar careers in film and television and bolster our country's standing across the planet. Why, then, have they not been commissioning new work with the same ambitious reach? We must not allow new writing for the theatre to retreat into a narrow political and aesthetic ghetto the Monsterists helped drag it from nearly twenty years ago. Programming must be bold in content as well as form, diverse in political attitude as well as personnel. There's nothing drearier for an audience than art made for political reasons and nothing more exciting than finding the political in art. And if we carry on down this road of theatre being tribal, being the territory of a group of social engineers, we'll weaken it's power at a time when we need it most.

There's always been, in UK theatre, an umbilical connection between the subsidised and the commercial. Do we blink when we see one of our great tragedians pop up in an *Avengers* movie or chewing the scenery on *Midsomer Murders*? No. Do we find it odd that a controversial new play that started life in a small, scrappy, subsidised upstairs room might find its way to an 800-seat West End theatre? No. This feels as natural to us as breathing and it's one of the reasons British theatre's regarded so highly.

But in this new world, when the old certainties are shattered, when all of these structures are creaking, we're going to have to rely on our writers to re-imagine the world anew. We're going to have to empower writers of all stripes to reach deeper and see further: to swim against the tide, to be pioneers. If it is to survive, theatre must place itself right at the heart of our society. It must explore the defining issues of our day in depth and with brutal honesty and unify human beings in a collective experience. Its writers must engage with the political and social complexities and contradictions of our time and not just the ones that won't get them into trouble.

We're all flawed. We all have a fractured sense of ourselves: we all have obstacles to overcome and advantages to capitalise on. We've all had broken hearts and little victories. We have complicated families and combative relationships. We judge each other quickly and on very flimsy evidence. We don't see the whole picture. We sin. We covet. We cheat. We lust. We curse. We think ill of people. We generalise about them. If we don't write about these things, we are not being honest about the human condition.

Perhaps I'm out of step. I do like old things. I like things you can hold in your hand and feel the heft of. I like things that have been around for a long time, that were made to last. I like old buildings in old streets in old cities. I like old films and old books and old music. I like classic cooking and ancient civilisations and ancient wisdom. I like old people and their old stories. I like old values of decency and civility and tolerance. If you don't like old things, you don't belong in the theatre. The theatre is as old as it gets. If you don't want to connect to a group of strangers who are different from you, you don't belong in the theatre. If you want to be a politician or a journalist or a social worker or a lecturer, go, by all means, and work in those fields. The theatre is a place for artists. If you don't have, at the very least, buried somewhere deep inside you, an optimistic and eternal faith in the potential of human beings to confront their flaws and to change, then you have no business in the theatre. If you're intolerant of the dark and the rough and the crude and the offensive, please use social media and stay away from the stage. If you want to write, be in the world. Speak to people who are different from you, speak to people who don't agree with you: find out why they think the way they think and behave the way they behave, listen to them, even if you don't like what they have to say. It will make you a better writer.

Some events are so immense they have the effect of shifting humanity on its axis. Every few generations a global crisis comes along that is so overwhelming it galvanises the whole of humankind, forces it to reassess and realign, to make acute and rapid adjustments, to adapt or die. It's a reckoning. And while there've always been great leaps forward in human innovation – the invention of the wheel and the printing press, the discovery of the double helix, the development of the pill, the construction of the World Wide Web – there are also times like these. Times of destruction, times of sickness and trembling and death that can completely change the way we see ourselves. In these times, history becomes present, becomes something we live and breathe. Sometimes these emergencies come like tidal waves to sweep away the old order and usher in the new. These are the kinds of catastrophes to tear holes in the fabric of our civilisation, to carve wounds so deep they can never be repaired: to create whole new realities. It's a moment of profound transition. And to cope with it a new psychological and social landscape emerges. There was a time before and there is a time after. What we do in the next few years will define an era.

In the years after the Second World War, British theatre produced Beckett, Bond, Delaney, Dunbar, Osborne, Orton, Pinter, Wesker, on and on and on: writers who burned with passion, writers who tore down the old structures, writers who made yowling, furious art that was unthinkable a generation before, writers who changed the landscape of our culture totally, who changed how we understood our own humanity. What new energy will be injected into our writers after this calamity? What new living cathedrals of imagination will be thrown up?

Victory against the virus will be signified by the full and fearless reopening of our theatres. The triumph of a healthy society will be the way it supports these theatres and their artists and how free they feel to respond to the world. In return it will be the solemn duty of playwrights to reach out to all people and to reconnect to our common humanity. 'We've got to live', writes Lawrence, 'no matter how many skies have fallen'.

A surgeon friend of mine recently expressed concern that the cure we were imposing on the population during the Covid crisis might turn out to be worse than the disease. He saw cancer and cardiac wards empty, people scared of reporting symptoms and getting early diagnoses. He saw a future epidemic of mental health problems and economic collapse. At some point we'll have to stem the bleeding. As a doctor he knows better than most that there is no life without risk. The theatre can lead the way in our cultural recovery, but there is no recovery without intervention and effort, without pain and risk.

With the old world collapsing beneath us every day, what will we build together in ruins? In the aftermath of the Trump victory, the Public Theatre took Lynn Nottage's *Sweat* out to the steel towns and the Rust Belt and played it on a bare set – a few chairs and tables – in town halls and community spaces. Perhaps there's a leaner, more malleable theatre to be conceived of in the new era. Perhaps we need to reimagine our art form as something unadorned, but teeming with inner life: the actors, the words and the audience. That's all we really need. So long as the words light a fire under us. Theatre, like surgery, can be a scarring, bruising business. I'm the first to admit my plays have bothered people, bored them, enraged them, failed them. I've seen people walk out before the end, disgusted, frustrated. I saw one noted director red-faced, inflamed with outrage, stomping around in the green room afterwards demanding to know what right I had to write *that* play about *those* people.

What right? Make it work dramatically and you have every right. I'd go further and say you have an absolute duty to set the cat among the pigeons, to cause trouble, to air the unpopular view. This is why our role in society is so absolutely essential, particularly at a time when nuance and controversy are under threat.

It isn't always a battle. I've been fortunate enough to sit in rooms with prodigiously gifted artists bringing my work to life. I've travelled halfway across the world and up and down the country to see productions of my plays. I've seen my plays in print, and occasionally I've seen them being studied and re-imagined. I've seen a room full of strangers rocking with laughter or moved to tears or cheering with recognition. For those rare and precious times I've connected with that group of strangers, Timberlake, yes, I think I'd still begin. For the times I've been able to help others to access their voice, incite them to write, yes I'd still do it.

When you start to make art, the world moves quickly to try to limit you. To put you into a box and insist you stay there. Resist. That's what writing is. An act of resistance. Each new play is an act of belligerent defiance. It's an uneasy life and requires significant reserves of inner steel. You're embarking on a career that's full of pitfalls and phenomenally precarious. Everywhere you look there will be voices disparaging you, or blocking you or undermining you, not to mention your own inner voice doing all those things ten times worse. Your job is to defy those voices. To defy the common will. You must bore down into human experience, cut out the viscera and hold it up for all to see. Force them to look. Your job is to find a deeper truth and confront the world with it, even when it doesn't want to listen.

When a playwright is able to distil a universal truth about the human condition into two hours of stage traffic, they can produce work that penetrates the collective unconscious and remains long after the production has evaporated into dust. A play that stands completely on its own terms, that comes alive on stage, that has an audience rapt, or enraged, or moved is, for me, an enduring miracle of human invention.

If we want a theatre that truly connects, it cannot confine itself to a single aesthetic, or to a single political orthodoxy. An idea is a network. An argument only breaks through if it combines watertight logic with human emotion.

To write is to cross the divide. We must cover the distance between thought and action, between text and audience, between radicalism and complacency, between *us* and *them*: only then can we truly smash through the stasis. You'll never write something true if it follows a formula, or if it doesn't deviate from the received wisdom. You'll never write something enduring if you don't set your face against the expectations of the world. Because in the face of the widening divides in our political and cultural life, what else can we do but embrace the contradictions and diversity of human behaviour, and when faced with mob mentality, with duplicity and simplicity and stupidity, what else can we do but resist?